Swift

Programming

Nuts and bolts

Motu Presse   Keith Lee

Swift Programming *Nuts and bolts*

ISBN (pbk): 978-0-6925-5289-6
ISBN (electronic): 978-1-4951-6856-7

The source code for examples that accompany this book, as well as other resources, is available at www.motupresse.com.

Contents

Preface

Swift is a new programming language created specifically for developing applications targeted for the iOS, watchOS, and OS X platforms. It was designed to make programming both simpler and more fun; as such it includes a number of features that make it easier to create fast, safe, and robust applications. With the 2.0 release of Swift and its subsequent open-source distribution, the use and popularity of the language will only continue to grow.

Swift Programming *Nuts and bolts* provides a clear and concise overview of the programming language, describes its key features and APIs, and presents recommendations for developing iOS, watchOS, and OS X apps using Swift. Very quickly, the reader will have a solid understanding of Swift and be ready to begin using it on his/her projects.

So, *let's begin!*

INTRODUCTION

Swift is a new, modern programming language for developing applications for the Apple iOS, watchOS, and OS X platforms. As you are probably well aware, these platforms are some of the most popular application development environments. In fact, well over one million iOS apps have been developed and distributed to the Apple App Store. General users and IT professionals alike want to be able to quickly grasp the fundamentals of this technology and begin using it to build apps. This book was written to help you acquire this knowledge by answering the following questions: 1) **What** are the general features and purpose of Swift, 2) **Why** should you use it (versus other programming languages), and 3) **How** do you quickly begin developing apps with Swift? This book provides these answers.

Who This Book Is For

Swift Programming *Nuts and bolts* is for developers of all levels of expertise who have, at a minimum, knowledge of basic programming concepts. In addition knowledge of functional and/or object-oriented programming concepts, while not necessary, is also useful.

What You Need

Before you begin writing Swift code for the Apple platforms, you'll need an Intel-based Mac computer running OS X El Capitan (version 10.11) or later. You'll also need Xcode 7 (or later), Apple's toolset for iOS, watchOS, and OS X software development using Swift 2.

How to Use This Book

This book is divided into 14 chapters. Chapters 1 through 4 focus on the fundamental building blocks of Swift. **Chapter 1** provides a high-level overview of language and summarizes its key features. In **Chapter 2** you'll learn about variables and assignments, language-defined operators, and how to create common expressions and statements. **Chapter 3** provides an overview of the key safe programming elements of the Swift programming language, and shows how they can be used to make your programs more reliable and bug-free. **Chapter 4** covers the Swift constructs for controlling when parts of a program are executed and how many times

Chapters 5 through 9 build on this introduction by covering Swift's fundamental abstractions for building programs of arbitrary complexity. **Chapter 5** provides an overview of the Swift Standard Library, a collection of reusable software resources (data types, functions, etc.) available across the language implementation. It includes a detailed overview of the

Standard Library numeric types, strings, collections, and several of its more common built-in functions. Swift provides support for the creation of *tuples*, an ordered list of elements, which can be of any type. **Chapter 6** provides an overview of tuples and shows how you can use them in your code. A Swift *function* is a named, self-contained group of code that performs a specific task. **Chapter 7** shows you how to develop and use functions. **Chapter 8** provides an introduction to *closures*, an unnamed, self-contained group of code that performs a specific task and also allows access to variables outside of their typical scope. A *named type* is a user-defined type that is composed of both data and methods for operating on this data. In **Chapter 9** you'll learn how to create and use the enumeration, structure, class, and protocol named types.

Chapters 10 through 12 cover more advanced features of Swift. **Chapter 10** examines extensions, a language mechanism for adding new functionality (i.e. types, methods, etc.) to an existing enumeration, structure, class, or protocol. *Generic programming* is an advanced feature that enables you to create software that's parameterized with respect to types. **Chapter 11** shows you how to create and use Swift generic functions and types. Swift provides language-level mechanisms that enable you to detect, report, and handle errors. In **Chapter 12** you'll learn how to implement your code to manage runtime error conditions using the Swift error handling APIs.

Chapters 13-14 conclude this book with an overview of tools you can use to get help while programming with Swift, a list of references to resources and documentation available on the programming language, and pointers to additional topics you'll want to explore as you gain more experience.

Typographical Conventions

The following typographical conventions are used in this book:

Bold font style within the body of text indicates significant words or phrases. Bold is also used to identify chapters or sections within a chapter.

Italics font style indicates new words or phrases that are explained further in the body of the book.

`Monospaced, constant width` font is used for programming code excerpts and examples.

`Monospaced, constant width bold` font is used within programming code excerpts and examples to indicate key elements and concepts.

Monospaced, constant width italic font is used within programming code excerpts to indicate comments.

Attention New Programmers!

Particularly for beginners, computer programming can be a little frustrating at first. Here are a few recommendations that will be very helpful when you start writing programs with Swift:

Proper syntax - It is **very** important that your program code has the correct syntax. Specifically, capitalization, spacing, and other syntax elements should be identical to that shown in this book and the reference documentation. In general computers and programming languages are very strict about syntax, so if you make typing errors your program will not run properly.

Check your work – Mistakes happen, so check your work frequently, particularly just before you run your programs.

One step at a time – Develop your programs incrementally. This means write small portions of code, test and fix errors until you verify the code works as expected, and add more code to your program accordingly.

Chapter **1**

GETTING STARTED

During the 2014 Apple Worldwide Developer Conference (WWDC) the Swift programming language was introduced. This announcement took the developer community by complete surprise, and promised to change how applications are developed for the Apple platforms. At its release Apple stated that Swift would make it easier for developers to create apps, and that it incorporates many of the best features of modern programming languages. Now this all sounds nice and makes for good sound bites, but what does this really mean for you as a developer? In this chapter we'll attempt to address these concerns by providing you a brief introduction to the Swift platform, and then help you *get your feet wet* by guiding you through the creation of your first Swift program.

Key Features

What makes Swift such a great programming language, and why should you learn it? After all there are literally thousands of programming languages to choose from, and many of you reading this book already have experience with one or more. In fact some of you may already use Objective-C, which up to now has been the primary programming language used for Apple software development. Well, the reasons Swift is such a compelling choice for developing your next app include the following:

Safety - Swift has been designed with safety in mind. Specifically the language adopts many safe programming practices (e.g. type safety, automatic memory management, required variable initialization, overflow checks, etc.). This enables you to develop more robust, reliable apps.

Speed - The Swift platform provides numerous optimizations to improve application performance. Compiled Swift code, the Swift Standard Library, and even the language itself are optimized. As a result, with Swift you will develop better performing, more responsive apps.

Efficiency - Swift takes the best features of C and Objective-C, and adds modern features from a variety of contemporary programming languages. In addition Swift includes a whole range of new and powerful language constructs that enable you to more naturally and efficiently develop software. You'll find as a developer that, in many cases, what would take many lines of code in Objective-C can be done with far fewer in Swift, without sacrificing readability. Hence Swift makes it both easier and quicker for you to develop great apps.

1

Ease-of-Use - The Swift platform has multiple features that make it easy to both learn the language and/or migrate existing applications over time. This greatly reduces the barrier of entry for learning Swift along with the cost of adoption. In addition Apple has created *playgrounds*, an interactive environment for programming with Swift. Code entered into a playground file is compiled and run in real-time as you type, with the results of operations presented in a step-by-step timeline as they execute. This makes playgrounds a great tool for learning and experimenting with Swift. Swift is also designed to be interoperable with your existing iOS and OS X apps; Swift code is compiled with the Apple LLVM compiler and executed with the Objective-C runtime. As a result, these apps will continue to work *"as-is"*. You can also use C, Objective-C, and Swift code in the same program, thus enabling you to convert existing software to Swift incrementally, over time.

Development Tools

Apple provides developer tools (i.e. software libraries and a developer toolkit) that you will use for Swift application development. The Software Development Kits (SDKs) are comprised of Application Programmer Interfaces (APIs) and services. The iOS SDK includes APIs and services for developing iOS apps, WatchKit includes APIs and services for developing Apple watchOS apps, while the OS X SDK includes APIs and services for developing OS X apps.

Xcode is a complete developer toolkit for building iPhone, iPad, Mac, and Apple Watch apps. It is fully integrated with each SDK and includes all the tools necessary for writing and compiling source code, developing graphical user interfaces, software testing and debugging, release build and version management, project management, and other features. Xcode includes the Xcode Integrated Development Environment (IDE), Interface Builder for creating user interfaces, the LLVM compiler, the LLDB source code debugger, along with full support for Swift 2 (Xcode 7 and above).

Xcode is a free download for all members of the Apple Developer Program. If you are not a member of the program, it is also available as a free download from the Mac App Store. Xcode 7 will run on any Mac computer that has OS X El Capitan (version 10.11) or later installed.

Your First Swift Program

OK, so now that we have completed the introduction you're going to develop your first Swift program! First download and install Xcode 7 as described in the previous paragraph. Once this is done, launch Xcode and you should observe the Xcode welcome window as shown in Figure 1-1.

Figure 1-1. Xcode Welcome Window

Note: If you have an iOS device (e.g., iPhone/iPad) connected to your computer, you may see a message asking whether or not you want to use that device for development. Because we will not be developing a mobile app for this program, you should click the **Ignore** button.

This screen presents you with a variety of options: create a new project, open an existing project, and so forth. Because you want to create a new application, select the **Create a new Xcode project** option (you can also do this by selecting **New > Project...** from the Xcode File menu). The Xcode workspace window will be displayed followed by the New Project Assistant pane on top of that, as shown in Figure 1-2.

Figure 1-2. Xcode New Project Assistant

The left side of the New Project Assistant is divided into iOS, watchOS, and OS X sections. You are going to start off by creating a command line application, so select **Application** under the OS X section. In the upper-right pane you'll see several icons that represent each of the project templates that are provided as starting points for creating OS X applications, select **Command Line Tool** and click **Next**. The *Project Options* window will be displayed (in Figure 1-3) for you to input project-specific information.

Figure 1-3. Xcode Project Options Window

Specify the *Product Name* for the project (for this example **Greetings**), an *Organization Name* (the name for the organization of the project, in this example **Swift Programming**), an *Organization Identifier* (this is a name used to provide an identifier for your application, typically you input something like your domain name in reverse order but any name will suffice), and the programming *Language* of the application (Xcode supports various programming languages, including Swift and Objective-C, here we select **Swift**). After this information has been provided click the **Next** button and the window shown in Figure 1-4 is displayed for entering the name and location of your project.

Figure 1-4. Xcode Project Location Window

Specify the location in your file system where you want the project to be created (if necessary select **New Folder** and enter the name and location for the folder); also be sure to uncheck the **Source Control** checkbox. After this has been entered click the **Create** button and the workspace window is opened.

Xcode Workspace

The workspace window is divided into a toolbar that extends horizontally across the top of the window and three areas below it divided into columns that take up the remainder of the window.

The toolbar includes controls to start and stop running your project (the **Run** and **Stop** buttons), a popup menu to select the **Scheme** you want to run, the **Activity View** in the middle of the toolbar, a set of **Editor** buttons, and a set of **View** buttons. The three areas below the toolbar comprise the *Navigator* area, *Editor* area, and *Utility* area. The navigator area is used to view and access different resources (files, etc.) within a project. The editor area is where you'll actually write most of your program. The utility area is used to view and access Help and other inspectors and to use ready-made resources in your project. This is a (very) high-level overview of the elements that comprise the Xcode workspace, so don't worry about understanding all of this right now; you will gain plenty of experience using Xcode and its associated tools as you develop code throughout this book.

Greetings Earthlings!

You have now created an Xcode project named **Greetings**. If you look at the navigator area of the workspace window, at the top you'll see a selector bar comprised of seven buttons and below that the main navigator area. Click the leftmost button (a folder icon) to see the *Project Navigator* view. The project navigator shows the contents (files, resources, etc.) of a project or Xcode workspace. Now open the **Greetings** folder by clicking the disclosure triangle alongside the Greetings folder icon. In the folder select the file named `main.swift`; the template code created by Xcode for this file is shown in Figure 1-5.

Figure 1-5. Xcode Greetings Project

Yes this is the ubiquitous "Hello, World!" program; when you create a Swift command line program with Xcode it creates a `main.swift` file that includes the default code shown in Figure 1-5. The code consists of an `import` directive

```
import Cocoa
```

and a single program statement

```
print("Hello, World!")
```

An `import` directive is used to make a software library available for use in your program; in this case the statement imports the Cocoa Framework libraries, including the Swift Standard Library APIs. The program statement uses the Swift Standard Library `print(_:)` function to print the text supplied within the parentheses (surrounded by double-quotes) to the *Output Pane* (located below the editor area). *Note: don't worry too much about the details right now, you'll learn all about Swift functions and the Standard Library in upcoming chapters.* Now let's modify the greeting; in the Editor area change the greeting text as follows.

```
print("Hello World, Welcome to Swift!")
```

Now compile and run this program now by clicking the Run button in the toolbar (or selecting **Run** from the Xcode Product menu). The *Output Pane* (located below the editor area) shown in Figure 1-6 displays the message `Hello World, Welcome to Swift!`.

Figure 1-6. Hello World, Welcome to Swift!

Perfect, you have learned how to create an Xcode project and also compile and run a simple Swift program. Feel free to continue exploring the Xcode workspace window to become more familiar with its contents.

Using Playgrounds

Earlier in this chapter we made note of playgrounds, the interactive programming environment for Swift. Now in the previous section you learned how to code and run a Swift program and this was pretty cool, but to be honest it may seem like a lot of hoops to jump through just to see the results of what you coded. Swift playgrounds are meant to address this by enabling you to enter code and interactively see your results. This is great for learning Swift, exploring its standard libraries, and general experimenting. To illustrate this, now you're going to create a Swift playground and take it out for a test drive.

Launch Xcode again, and this time when the Welcome Window (see Figure 1-1) is displayed select the **Get started with a playground** option (you can also do this by selecting **New > Playground...** from the Xcode File menu). A window will be displayed for entering playground options, as shown in Figure 1-7.

Figure 1-7. Playgrounds Options Window

Specify the *Name* for your playground (here I entered
SwiftProgramming), for the *Platform* select **OS X**, and finally click the
Next button. The window shown in Figure 1-8 is displayed for entering the
location and group of your playground.

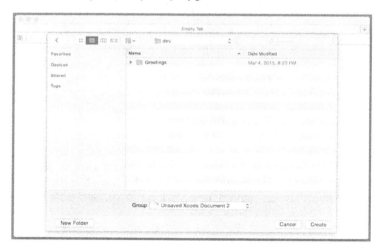

Figure 1-8. Playgrounds Location Window

Specify the location in your file system where you want the playground to
be created (if necessary select **New Folder** and enter the name and
location for the folder; you may want to save your playground to the
Desktop for ease of access), leave the *Group* as **Unsaved Xcode
Document 2**, and click the **Create** button. In Xcode a new playground file
called *SwiftProgramming.playground* is created and the Playground

Window shown in Figure 1-9 is displayed.

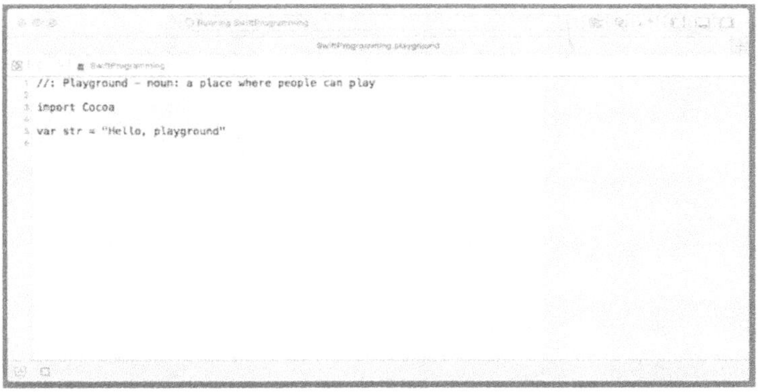

Figure 1-9. Playground Window

Xcode Playground Window

An Xcode Playground Window is divided into a workspace toolbar that extends horizontally across the top of the window and several areas below it divided into columns that take up the remainder of the window. Figure 1-9 displays: 1) the **Source Editor** window where you type in Swift code, and 2) the **Results** sidebar that executes and displays the results of the code written in window. When you finish typing code in the window or take a pause, Xcode calculates and displays the results in the sidebar. Note that results in the sidebar may temporarily change from black to gray while Xcode recalculates them. If you make a mistake, Xcode displays an error symbol (an exclamation point icon) in the gutter located alongside the Source Editor window. Click the symbol to see an explanation of the mistake. After you correct or remove the mistake, Xcode redisplays the results of your valid code.

Welcome to Swift Playgrounds!

As shown in Figure 1-9, the template code generated when the new playground was created includes a comment string, an import directive, and a single program statement that assigns the text string *Hello, playground* to a variable named `str`.

The results sidebar displays the results of the variable assignment, e.g. the value for the variable `str`. Let's change the value for this variable by modifying it as follows:

```
var str = "Hello, Swift Playgrounds"
```

Observe (in Figure 1-10) below how the value in the sidebar has been updated.

Figure 1-10. Hello Swift Playgrounds

As this example demonstrates, interactive playgrounds are a great tool for learning and experimenting with Swift. In fact, you'll use them throughout this book to demonstrate Swift language features.

Chapter **2**

BASIC ELEMENTS

Fundamentally a computer program is comprised of data and operations on this data. As such, all programming languages have a number of basic structural elements that are used to write data and the corresponding operations in source code. These elements include variables, operators, and expressions. In this chapter you'll learn how to code these in Swift.

Variables

In Figure 1-10 you wrote the following code to declare a variable and assign it a value:

```
var str = "Hello, Swift Playgrounds"
```

Now you are going to learn more about variables in Swift. In computer science, a *variable* is a named reference to a storage location. Variables are used in a program to store, update, and retrieve data. Swift provides the `var` keyword for declaring a variable by name, aka an *identifier*. A Swift identifier begins with either a letter or an underscore, followed by any combination of underscores, letters, and numbers. The letters of an identifier are case sensitive; Swift also supports most Unicode characters for its identifiers. The following are examples of valid variable names:

```
greeting
```

```
_myNumber
```

```
pi_π
```

Notice that the last example variable, `pi_π`, includes a Unicode character (π), highlighting the language's support for Unicode. A Swift variable also has a data type, meaning only certain kinds of data can be stored in it. Swift supports a variety data types, including simple data types such as integers and floating-point numbers, composite data types that contain multiple types, and function types that represent the type of a function. A variable's type can be either *inferred,* whereby the Swift compiler automatically figures out its type based on context, or explicitly specified with a Swift *type annotation*. For variables a type annotation is written directly after the variable name with a colon followed by a space and then the name of the type. The following example declares several variables with corresponding type annotations:

```
var greeting: String
```

```
var _myNumber: Int
```

The first statement above declares a variable named greeting of type string (a sequence of characters), whereas the second declares a variable named _myNumber of integer type. Swift also enables you to create *constant* variables - variables whose value cannot be changed once set. The let keyword is used for declaring a constant variable. The corresponding value of a constant must be assigned before it is used. The following example declares and sets a value to a constant variable named LuckyNumber7:

```
let LuckyNumber7 = 7
```

Storing a value that will not change as a constant reduces programming errors and also enables the Swift compiler to perform optimizations that can improve performance. Thus you should only store a value as a variable if it may change. Now when should you explicitly declare a type (via a type annotation) versus using type inference? For variables that are declared and initialized at the same time, Swift can almost always determine the correct type based on the value supplied. This reduces the amount of code you have to write; hence if possible you should use type inference whenever declaring and initializing variables. The following example demonstrates type inference in action.

```
var greeting = "Hello, Swift Playgrounds!"
var _myNumber = 21
let isSwiftCool = true
```

The variable greeting is correctly inferred to be of string type, the variable _myNumber is inferred to be of integer type, and the constant isSwiftCool is inferred to be of Boolean type.

A Note About Literals

In the previous examples variables are initialized with *literal* values. A Swift literal can be defined as the representation in source code of the value of a type. Now the representation is a function of the variable's type. For example Swift numeric literals are represented in code with their numeric literal values (e.g. 21 in the above example). A Swift string literal is written as a sequence of characters surrounded by double quotes. A Swift Boolean literal is written as a value of either true or false. You will learn how to code other Swift literals later in this book.

Comments

Comments provide a mechanism for documenting code in order to facilitate comprehension by anyone who needs to read it. Swift provides mechanisms to support both single line and multi-line comments.

Single Line Comments

The `//` marker identifies text following (on the same line) as comment text; it will be ignored by the compiler. The marker can be placed anywhere on a line, hence single line comments provide a good mechanism for describing what that particular line of code does. The following example includes a single line comment at the end of a line.

```
print("Hello, World!")        // Print message
```

Multi-Line Comments

Comments that extend over multiple lines use the markers `/*` and `*/` respectively. Everything between these two markers is considered a comment and is ignored by the compiler, regardless of where the markers appear on a line. Here is an example multi-line comment.

```
/*
 * This is a multi-line comment
 */
```

Operators

In Swift an operator is a language-defined symbol or phrase that can be used to perform a specific *operation* on one or more variables and/or expressions. Swift's basic operators support assignment, arithmetic, bitwise, comparison, and Boolean operations.

Assignment Operator

The assignment operator assigns the result of a value on the right side of the assignment symbol (=) to the variable to the left of the symbol. The constant or variable (to the left of the assignment symbol) must have the same type as the value being assigned to it. The assignment operator is *binary* because it has an *operand* (i.e., data on which the operation is performed) on each side of the operator. The following code provides an example use of the Swift assignment operator.

```
var str = "Hello, Swift Playgrounds"
```

The assignment operator does not return a value; this prevents errors when it is accidently coded in an expression where the Boolean equal to (==) operator is intended.

Arithmetic Operators

The Swift arithmetic operators are binary operators that perform arithmetic calculations. Multiple arithmetic operators can be used in a single expression. By default Swift does not allow values to overflow from an arithmetic calculation, and an arithmetic operator does not return a value. Swift supports four standard arithmetic operations: addition (+), subtraction (-), multiplication (*), and division (/). Swift also supports the *modulo* (i.e. remainder) operator (%); it is used to return the remainder left over when performing division on two values. The remainder operator works for both integer and floating-point values.

By default the Swift arithmetic operators do not overflow; as a result an overflow condition when performing an arithmetic operation results in a program error. Swift includes an additional set of operators that provide overflow behavior. These operators begin with an ampersand and allow you to perform overflow addition (&+), subtraction (&-), and multiplication (&*), truncating the value when the result overflows.

Increment/Decrement Operators

These unary arithmetic operators are used to increment (++) or decrement (--) the value of a numeric value by 1. Either operator can be placed before (pre-increment/decrement) or after (post-increment/decrement) the variable name. If an increment/decrement operator is placed before the variable name its value is incremented or decremented *before* any other operations are performed on the variable and the result returned. Conversely, post-increment/decrement causes the value of the variable to be incremented or decremented *after* the result is returned. These operators can be used on any integer or floating-point type.

Now let's experiment with the Swift arithmetic operators. In Xcode open the **SwiftProgramming** playground, delete any existing code, and then add the following statements:

```
var product = 3 * 4
var series = 1 + 2 + 3 + 5 + 8
```

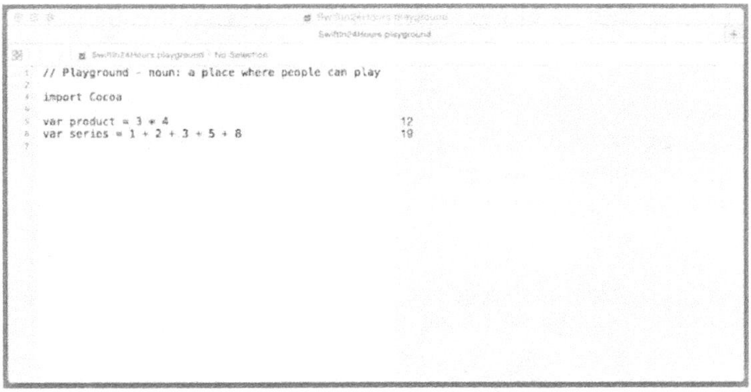

Figure 2-1. Experimenting with Arithmetic Operators

As shown in Figure 2-1, the first statement computes the value of the variable `product` using the multiplication operator, while the second statement computes the value of the variable `series` using the arithmetic operator. Note from this example that multiple operations can be combined in a single statement. Now let's demonstrate the increment operator. Add the following statements:

```
var counter = 0

var totalCount = ++counter
```

The increment operator is placed before the variable `totalCount`, thus it is assigned the value of the variable `counter` after it is incremented by 1. Verify the sidebar displays that the value of `totalCount` equals 1. Now change the statement to perform a post-increment (i.e., move the increment operator after the variable `counter`) and observe the sidebar displays that the value of `totalCount` equals 0.

Bitwise Operators

The bitwise operators enable bitwise operations on binary numbers. Any decimal number can be represented as a binary number. The bitwise operators are of two types: comparison and shift. The bitwise comparison operators can perform bit-by-bit comparisons of two numbers, and shifts of each bit in a binary number. These operators return a binary number consistent with the operation. The bitwise shift operators shift each bit in a binary number the specified number of positions.

The bitwise **AND** (`&`) operator uses the AND operation to perform a bit-by-bit comparison of two numbers. In each position of the binary sequence for the two numbers an AND operation is performed; if both bits are 1 then a 1 is set in the same position of the resulting number, else a zero is set.

For example a bitwise AND operation on the following two numbers (14 [binary 1110], and 13 [binary 1101]) would yield a binary result of 1100 (12 in decimal).

The bitwise **OR** (|) operator uses the OR operation to perform a bit-by-bit comparison of two numbers; it sets a 1 in the same position of the resulting number if there is a one in that position for either (or both) operand.

The bitwise **XOR** (^) operator (also known as the exclusive OR) uses the XOR operation to perform a bit-by-bit comparison of two numbers; it sets a 1 in the same position of the resulting number if there is a one in that position for one and only one of the operands, otherwise the bit is set to 0.

The bitwise **left shift** (<<) operator moves each bit in a binary number the specified number of positions to the left. As the bits are shifted to the left, zeroes are placed in the right most (vacated) positions, and the left most (high order) bits are discarded if the shift exceeds the size of the variable containing the value.

The bitwise **right shift** (>>) operator moves each bit in a binary number the specified number of positions to the right. The right most (lower order) bits that are shifted off are discarded. The right shift is a *logical* right shift, because the left most (higher order) bit positions that have been vacated while right shifting are replaced with zeros.

The bitwise **one's complement** (~) operator is used to flip the bits of a binary number. Each bit of the number that is one is changed to a zero, and each bit that is a zero is changed to a one.

Let's experiment with the Swift bitwise operators. In Xcode re-open your playground (*SwiftProgramming.playground*), delete any existing code, and add the following statements:

```
var numAnd = 14 & 13
var numOr = 14 | 13
```

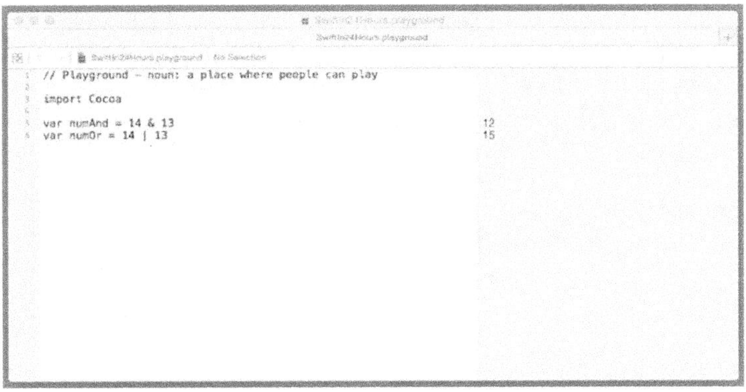

Figure 2-2. Experimenting with Bitwise Operators

Figure 2-2 demonstrates that a bitwise **AND** operation on the two numbers (14 [binary 1110], and 13 [binary 1101]) yields a binary result of 1100 (12 in decimal) as shown in the sidebar. A bitwise **OR** operation on the same numbers yields a binary result of 1111 (15 in decimal). Now let's use a bitwise shift operator; add the following statement:

```
var doubleSum = 14 << 1
```

Verify that a left shift of the number 14 (binary 1110) 1 bit to the left yields a value of 28 as shown in the sidebar.

Comparison Operators

The logical comparison operators perform a comparison of an expression and return a Boolean true or false value depending on the result of the comparison. These binary operators each require two operands. The basic Swift comparison operators are: *equal to* (==), *not equal to* (!=), *greater than* (>), *greater than or equal to* (>=), *less than* (<), and *less than or equal to* (<=).

The following example stores a Boolean value of true in the variable isGreaterNumber:

```
var n1 = 50
```

```
var n2 = 25
```

```
var isGreaterNumber = n1 > n2
```

Boolean Operators

The logical Boolean operators also return a Boolean true or false result; they differ from the comparison operators in that they take Boolean

values as operands. The Swift Boolean operators are logical **NOT** (!),
logical **AND** (&&), and logical **OR** (||). The logical **NOT** operator is unary;
it inverts a Boolean value sot that `true` becomes `false` and vice-versa.
The logical **AND** operator returns `true` if both of its operands are `true`,
else it returns `false`.

Let's experiment with the logical comparison and Boolean operators. In
your playground delete any existing code then add the following
statements:

```
var n1 = 50

var n2 = 25

var isGreaterAndPositive = (n1 > n2) && (n1 >= 0)
```

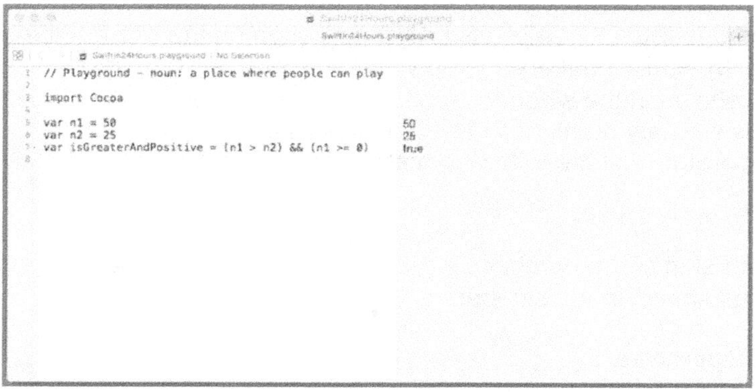

Figure 2-3. Experimenting with Logical Operators

As shown in Figure 2-3, this example combines both the *greater than or
equal to* operator and the logical **AND** operator, assigning the result to the
variable `isGreaterAndPositive`. Note that the operands for the logical
AND operation are both Boolean expressions.

Ternary Operator

The ternary operator provides a means of evaluating an expression as a
function of the evaluation of a Boolean condition. The syntax of the
operator is:

```
[condition] ? [true expression] : [false expression]
```

If the condition evaluates to `true` then the *true expression* is evaluated
and its result returned, otherwise the *false expression* is evaluated and its
result returned. In your playground delete any existing code then add the
following statements:

```
var number = 5
```

```
var numberSign = (number >= 0) ? "Positive" :
"Negative"
```

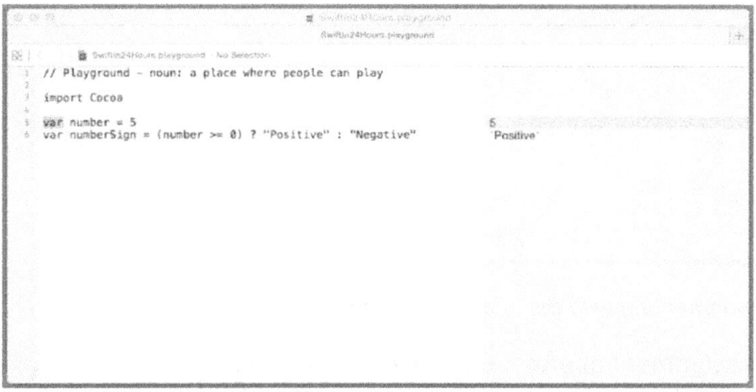

Figure 2-4. Experimenting with the Ternary Operator

Referring to Figure 2-4, the sidebar displays a value of `Positive` for the variable `numberSign`. Now change the value of `number` to -1; the sidebar should update to display a value of `Negative` for the variable `numberSign`.

Compound Assignment Operator

The Swift compound assignment operator combines an assignment with another operation. For example, the following statement increments the value of an integer variable named `mySum` by 2:

```
mySum = mySum + 2
```

The arithmetic assignment operator can be used to combine these assignment and addition operations into a single operation.

```
mySum += 2
```

Compound assignment can be used on the arithmetic, comparison, and bit-wise operators.

Let's experiment with the compound assignment operators. In your playground delete any existing code then add the following statements:

```
var doubleSum = 1
```

```
doubleSum += doubleSum
```

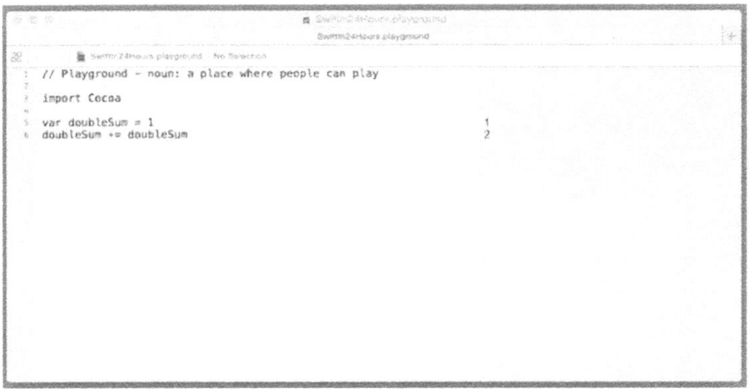

Figure 2-5. Experimenting with the Compound Assignment Operator

The addition assignment operator shown in Figure 2-5 correctly doubles the value of the variable and stores the result in the variable. You can achieve the same result by replacing the previous statement with the following using the multiplication assignment operator:

```
doubleSum *= 2
```

Verify that the sidebar computes the same result for the variable as shown in Figure 2-5. Now let's experiment with bitwise assignment operator. Replace the multiplication assignment operator statement with the following:

```
doubleSum <<= 1
```

Verify that the sidebar again computes the same result for the variable, effectively doubling the value of the variable `doubleSum`.

Expressions and Statements

An expression is a combination of values, variables, operators, and functions that are evaluated in order to produce another value, cause a side effect, or both. They can also be combined to create compound expressions. The following code lists examples of arithmetic, assignment, function call, and compound expressions:

```
3 * 4

var value = 3

print("Hello, World!")

3 * 4 + 5
```

In the case of compound expressions each programming language has specific rules of precedence and associativity that controls how each expression is evaluated. For example, the following code is a compound expression that groups two arithmetic expressions (addition and multiplication).

```
3 * 4 + 5
```

How should this expression be evaluated, as the result will be different depending upon whether the multiplication is done first or the addition is done first? The rules governing expression evaluation in these cases are known as the *operator precedence and associativity* rules. Swift operators are grouped together at different precedence levels. Operators of higher precedence are evaluated before operators of lower precedence. When operators at the same precedence level are found within a single expression, the corresponding *associativity* rule determines the order in which the operators are evaluated. The **Swift Programming Language Guide** details the operator precedence and associativity rules. To explicitly control the order of evaluation, your code should use parentheses to group expressions accordingly. The following code uses parentheses to insure that the addition is performed prior to multiplication:

```
3 * (4 + 5)
```

A statement is a unit of executable code. In Swift there are two kinds of statements - simple statements and control flow statements. Simple statements consist of either an expression or a declaration. For example, the following code consists of two simple statements that declare the variable sumProduct and compute a value for it:

```
var sumProduct: Int
sumProduct = 3 * (4 + 5)
```

Control flow statements are used to control the flow of program execution. Swift provides three types of control flow statements: loop statements, branch statements, and control transfer statements. Loop statements allow a block of code to be executed multiple times depending upon the loop condition. Swift has four loop statements: a for statement, a for-in statement, a while statement, and a repeat-while statement. Branch statements are used to execute certain parts of code depending on the value of one or more conditions. Swift has two branch statements: an if statement and a switch statement. Control transfer statements are used to change the order in which code is executed by unconditionally transferring execution to another block of code in a program. Swift has four control transfer statements: a break statement, a continue statement, a fallthrough statement, and a return statement.

In Swift by default a statement is closed on a new line, however the semicolon operator (;) can be used to group multiple statements on the same line. For example, the following code declares the variable `sumProduct` and then computes and stores a value for it on the same line:

```
var sumProduct: Int; sumProduct = 3 * (4 + 5)
```

Chapter 3

SAFE PROGRAMMING

Swift was designed with safety in mind; in fact a key objective during the development of the language was to make it easier for programmers to write safe, bug-free code. As such the Swift programming language adopts many safe-programming practices. In this chapter you will learn what these are and how to use them in your code.

Type Safety

A programming language's type safety can be considered the facilities it provides to prevent type errors, whereby a program attempts to perform operations on values that have the wrong data type. For example, attempting to add an integer and a string could generate a type error, resulting in incorrect program behavior.

Swift is primarily a *statically-typed* language; the compiler performs type checks when your code is compiled and flags any mismatched types as errors. This enables certain classes of bugs to be caught as early as possible in the development cycle, before program execution. Let's illustrate Swift static type checking in action with an example. In your playground delete any existing code then add the following statements:

```
var name = "Lucky"

var number = 7

var sum = name + number
```

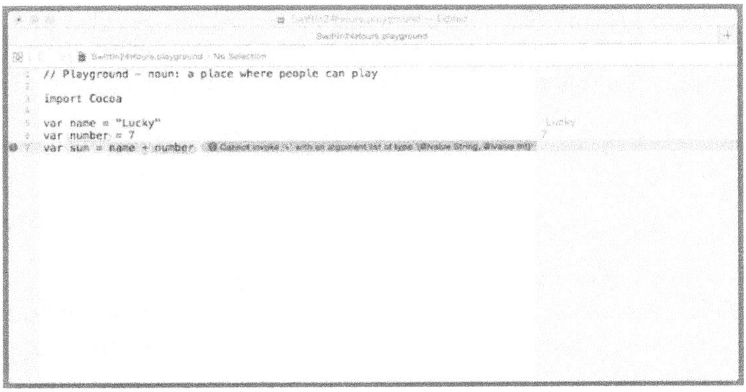

Figure 3-1. Swift Type Safety

The variable `name` is a string, while the variable `number` is an integer. As shown in Figure 3-1, when you attempt to add these two variables an error exclamation icon is displayed in the gutter. When you click on this icon you see displayed an error message specifying the type mismatch.

Swift type safety and type inference makes you more productive, by reducing the amount of code you have to write and also enabling you to catch and fix errors early in the development cycle.

Swift requires explicit conversions between variables and values of different types. It does not support automatic type conversion by the compiler, thereby preventing hidden conversion errors. For example, enter the following code in your playground:

```
var myNumber: Int = 25.321
```

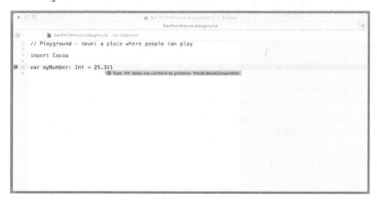

Figure 3-2. Swift Type Safety, Explicit Type Conversion

The variable `myNumber` is declared as an integer, yet it is being assigned a floating-point value. Figure 3-2 illustrates this is an attempt to perform an implicit conversion of the floating point value (25.321) to an integer. Swift will flag an error for this code specifying the type mismatch and indicating that an explicit type conversion must be performed. You must perform an explicit conversion of the value by creating a new variable of the desired type. This can be accomplished with the following code:

```
var myNumber: Int = Int(25.321)
```

As shown in the above code, a new integer is initialized with the input value (25.321), and an explicit type conversion is performed on the input value. As a result, the value is rounded to the nearest integer value and this result (25) is displayed in the sidebar.

Initialization

Improper or incomplete data initialization is a common source of program errors. Swift has several language mechanisms to prevent these when developing code. The language requires that every declared variable be initialized before it is used, and the compiler will flag an error if this has not been done. In addition, each constant must be assigned a corresponding value before data initialization has completed. Let's demonstrate this with an example; in your playground delete any existing code then add the following code:

```
var uninitialized: Double
uninitialized = uninitialized + 7
```

Figure 3-3. Swift Type Safety, Initialization

The error message shown in Figure 3-3 specifies that the variable has not been initialized before being used.

Swift includes language features that you can use to create one or more *initializers* for named data types. An initializer is a special method, automatically invoked when a named type (e.g. a structure, enumeration, or class) is created, that can be used to perform proper initialization of its variables. You will learn about initializers in the Named Types chapter.

Optionals

Earlier you read that variables are used in a program to store and/or return a value, and that Swift safe programming mechanisms enforce the initialization of every declared variable before it is used. However, what if you need to implement logic for a variable that has no value; how do you represent this in code? Many programming languages contain mechanisms for representing uninitialized, empty variables (i.e. variables with no value); however executing code that accesses such a variable can cause program errors.   Swift addresses this with the *optional* type, a mechanism that enables you to program uninitialized variables while still supporting safe programming practices.

An optional is a named type used to provide a value for a variable (if one exists) or nothing at all. Any Swift type can be declared as an optional type by appending the question mark (?) operator immediately after the type name. The following code declares an optional integer variable named `optionalInt` and (in the absence of a supplied initial value) automatically sets its value to `nil`.

```
var optionalInt: Int?
```

The Swift reserved word `nil` represents the absence of a value for an optional type. The next statement defines an optional variable named `greeting` that is initialized to the string *"Hello, World!"*.

```
var greeting: String? = "Hello, World!"
```

Swift provides several mechanisms for accessing the value of an optional type. If you know that the optional has a value, you can append the exclamation mark (!) operator immediately after its name to access its value. This is known as *forced unwrapping* of an optional's value. The following code uses forced unwrapping of the optional named `greeting` to print its value.

```
print(greeting!)
```

Forced unwrapping of an optional variable that does not have a value will cause a runtime error during program execution.

Optional Binding

Swift provides the *optional binding* mechanism to determine if an optional has a value and if so set a corresponding temporary variable to that value. Optional binding uses Swift conditional `if` and `while` statements to check if an optional has a value, and if so unwrap the value, assign it to a temporary value, and then execute the corresponding conditional logic. The syntax of optional binding for an `if` statement is depicted in the example of Listing 3-1.

Listing 3-1. Optional Binding if Statement

```
if let tempVar = optVar {
  // Conditional logic
}
```

As shown in Listing 3-1, the optional variable named `optVar` is checked to see if it contains a value. If it does, the value is assigned to the constant `tempVar` and the conditional logic enclosed within the curly braces is then executed.

Multiple simultaneous optional bindings can be provided in a single statement, each of which is separated by a comma. If any one of the optional bindings is not satisfied then the conditional logic is ignored. The syntax for multiple optional bindings is:

```
if let tempVar1=optVar1, ... tempVarN=optVarN {

  // Conditional logic

}
```

Each optional binding is evaluated in order. Optional bindings can also be paired with a `where` clause that is evaluated like a conditional `if` statement. The syntax for optional bindings with a `where` clause is:

```
if let tempVar1=optVar1 where tempVar1!=0 {

  // Conditional logic

}
```

Now let's illustrate use of optionals with an example. In your playground delete any existing code then add the following statements:

```
var greeting: String?

if var str = greeting {

  print(str)

}
```

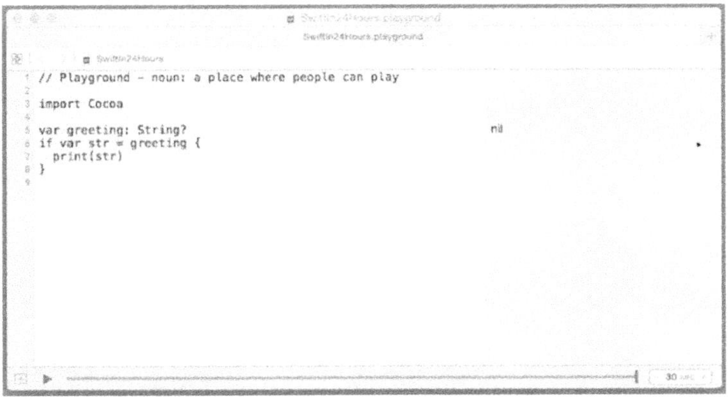

Figure 3-4. Optionals and Optional Binding

Referring to Figure 3-4, the sidebar displays no value for the variable `greeting`. As the variable has no value, it is not assigned to the temporary variable `str` and the conditional logic is not executed. Now let's change the definition of the optional `greeting` by assigning it a value:

```
var greeting: String? = "Hello World, Welcome to
Swift!"
```

Now in the sidebar observe that the variable `str` is assigned the value and that the conditional logic is executed, resulting in this string being printed to the console.

Memory Management

The overall quality of a program is often directly related to its management of system resources. A computer's operating system allocates a finite amount of main memory for program execution, and if a program attempts to use more memory than the amount allocated by the operating system, it will not operate correctly. Hence, a program should use only as much memory as needed, not allocate memory that it does not use, and not try to use memory that is no longer available. Swift provides automatic memory management in alignment with these goals.

During program execution Swift performs automatic memory management of class instances and closures; there are no special functions that you need to code for managing memory. Swift also provides language mechanisms that can be used to resolve *reference cycles* that can prevent proper memory management. You will learn more about using these mechanisms in the upcoming chapters on Swift *Closures* and *Named Types*.

Chapter **4**

CONTROL FLOW

Similar to many modern programming languages, Swift provides constructs that can be used to control the order and frequency of execution of different pieces of code. These are divided into several categories – 1) *conditional* constructs, 2) *loop* constructs, and 3) *transfer-of-control* constructs. In this chapter you'll learn about the features of the Swift control flow constructs and how to use them.

Conditionals

The conditional constructs enable you to execute blocks of code if a particular condition is met. Using Swift you implement these with `if` and `switch` statements. The `if` statement is most useful for coding logic that depends on simple conditions with only a few possible outcomes. The `switch` statement is ideal for complex conditions with multiple possible outcomes, and when pattern matching can be used to help select the appropriate block of code to execute.

If Statements

The `if` statement executes a block of code if a given Boolean conditional expression evaluates to `true`; otherwise it is skipped. In the previous chapter you used the `if` statement to perform *optional binding*; the general syntax of the Swift `if` statement is shown in Listing 4-1 below.

Listing 4-1. If Statement

```
if Conditional expression {

  // Conditional logic

}
```

The code that implements the conditional logic must be enclosed within braces; also the conditional expression can be enclosed within parentheses. Let's illustrate use of the `if` statement with an example; in your playground delete any existing code then add the following:

```
var number = 5

if (number % 2) == 0 {

  print("Even number")
```

}

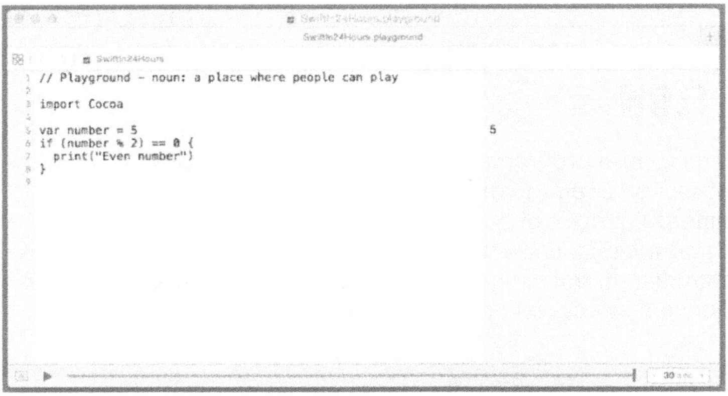

Figure 4-1. Using the If Statement

The code shown in Figure 4-1 determines whether the value of the remainder operator expression (number % 2) equals zero. If it does the conditional expression evaluates to `true` and the sidebar displays the text *Even number*. Change the value of the variable `number` to different even and odd integer numbers and verify the sidebar displays the text only when the variable is assigned an even value.

The Swift `else if` statement extends the `if` statement by enabling you to provide multiple conditional expressions, each with its corresponding block of code. The syntax of an `else if` statement is shown in Listing 4-2:

Listing 4-2. Else If Statement

```
if Conditional expression 1 {
  // Conditional logic
}
else if Conditional expression 2 {
  // Conditional logic
}
else if Conditional expression n {
  // Conditional logic
}
```

As with the `if` statement, the code accompanying each `else if` statement is surrounded by braces. Multiple `else if` statements can be chained together, each with its own corresponding block of code. The conditional expressions are evaluated sequentially and at most one of these branches will be executed (the first to evaluate to `true`); if none of the expressions evaluates to `true` then all of the branches are skipped. Let's illustrate use of these statements with an example; in your playground update your existing code as follows:

```
var number = 5
if (number % 2) == 0 {

   print("Even integer")

}
else if (number % 2) == 1 {

   print("Odd integer")

}
```

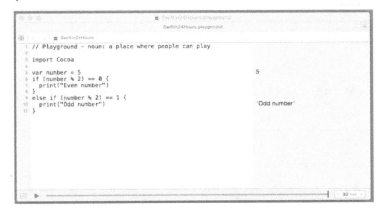

Figure 4-2. Using the Else If Statement

The code of Figure 4-2 includes two conditional expressions that are used to determine if the variable `number` is an even or odd integer value. It determines a number's parity by implementing the following logic: if the value of the remainder operator expression for the variable `(number % 2)` equals zero then the sidebar displays the text *Even number*, else if the value of the expression equals one then the sidebar displays the text *Odd number*. Change the value of the variable `number` to different even and odd positive numbers and verify the sidebar displays the correct text for each number.

Swift also provides an `else` statement that can be used to execute an alternative block of code if all of the accompanying conditional expressions evaluate to `false`. The syntax of the `else` statement is:

```
else {
  // Alternative code
}
```

As with the other conditional branches, braces surround the code accompanying the `else` statement. The `else` branch is always placed last (e.g. after the preceding `if` and `else if` branches). Let's illustrate this with an example; in your playground update your existing code as follows:

```
var number = 5
if (number % 2) == 0 {
  print("Even integer")
}
else if (number % 2) == 1 {
  print("Odd integer")
}
else {
  print("Floating-point number")
}
```

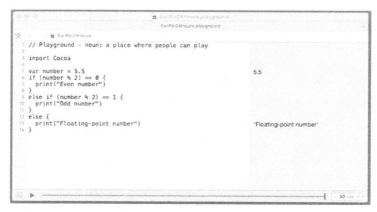

Figure 4-3. Using the Else Statement

As shown in Figure 4-3, an `else` branch is used to determine if the variable `number` is a floating-point number. This is the alternative case that will be executed if the variable `number` is set to a floating-point value (and hence the remainder operator returns a floating-point number). In this case the alternative code displays the text `Floating-point` `number`. Change the value of the variable to different integer and floating-point numbers and verify the sidebar displays the correct text for each number.

Switch Statement

The `if` statement works well for executing specific blocks of code depending on Boolean conditions, but what if you want to be able to control the execution of code based on a number of possibilities? The Swift `switch` statement provides this functionality; it enables conditional comparison and execution of code against a range of values and/or matching patterns. The `switch` statement matches against many kinds of data (numbers, strings, etc.) and also supports complex matching patterns (i.e. multiple values, ranges). The syntax for the `switch` statement is shown in Listing 4-3 below.

Listing 4-3. Switch Statement

```
switch control expression {
  case value 1:
    // Code executed for matching value 1
  case value 2, value 3:
    // Code executed for matching value 2 or value 3
  default:
    // Code executed if no matching value
}
```

The statement begins with the `switch` keyword, followed by a *control expression* or variable, then a set of switch cases enclosed by braces. Each case is declared using the `case` keyword, one or more values terminated with a colon, followed by the code to be executed if the case is matched. For the first found matching case value, the corresponding code is executed and the switch statement is exited. A switch statement must have a case for every possible matching control value; otherwise the compiler will flag an error. This can be accomplished by supplying a catchall case specified with the `default` keyword, which if present must be provided last as shown above. Multiple matching values are provided for a single case by separating each value (except the last) with a comma.

Now let's develop a simple example; in your playground delete any existing code then add the following:

```
var month: String = "January"
```

```
switch month {

    case "January", "March", "May", "July", "August",
"October", "December":

        print("There are 31 days in this month")

    case "April", "June", "September", "November":

        print("There are 30 days in this month")

    case "February":

        print("There are 28 or 29 days in this month")

    default:

        print("Please enter a valid month")

}
```

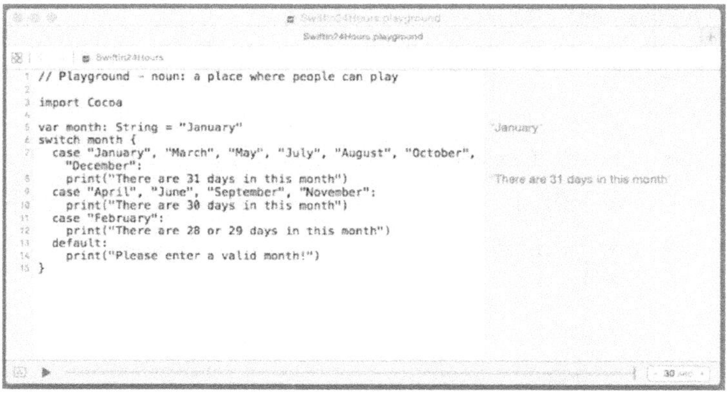

Figure 4-4. Using the Switch Statement

The code shown in Figure 4-4 has a switch with multiple cases that are used to display the number of days in the month. If the text provided for the variable is not as expected (i.e. the default case) then it displays a message requesting the user to enter a valid month. Change the variable `month` to different values (e.g., "February", "March", etc.) and verify the sidebar displays the correct text for each value.

A switch statement case can also check if a value falls within a specified interval. This is performed using the Swift *range operators;* these are used to express a range of numbers. The closed range operator (. . .) defines a range of numbers that runs sequentially from a beginning to an end number, including the beginning and ending values. The value of the beginning number cannot be greater than the ending. The syntax for the closed range operator is:

```
beginningNumber...endingNumber
```

The half-open range operator (..<) defines a range of numbers, similar to the closed range operator, but differing in that the range doesn't include the ending number. Its syntax is:

```
beginningNumber..<endingNumber
```

As mentioned above switch statements execute the first matching case and then transfer control to the code after the switch block; in other words it does not provide *fall-through* behavior, a feature of many other programming languages (such as C and Objective-C). If this behavior is needed the `fallthrough` keyword can be used. It should be coded at the end of the logic for each case that requires this behavior. The syntax for a switch statement that has a fall-through case is:

```
switch control expression {
    case value 1:
        // Code executed for matching value 1 with fall-
through
        fallthrough
    case value 2, value 3:
        // Code executed for matching value 2 or value 3
    default:
        // Code executed if no matching value
}
```

Now let's use the range operators in a switch statement: in your playground delete any existing code then add the following:

```
var testScore: UInt = 75
switch testScore {
    case 0..<60:
        print("Your grade is F, sorry!")
    case 60...69:
        print("Your grade is D")
    case 70...79:
        print("Your grade is C")
    case 80...89:
        print("Your grade is B, good job")
```

```
case 90...99:
    print("Your grade is A, outstanding")
case 100:
    print("Your grade is A+, perfect")
default:
    print("Please enter a valid test score")
}
```

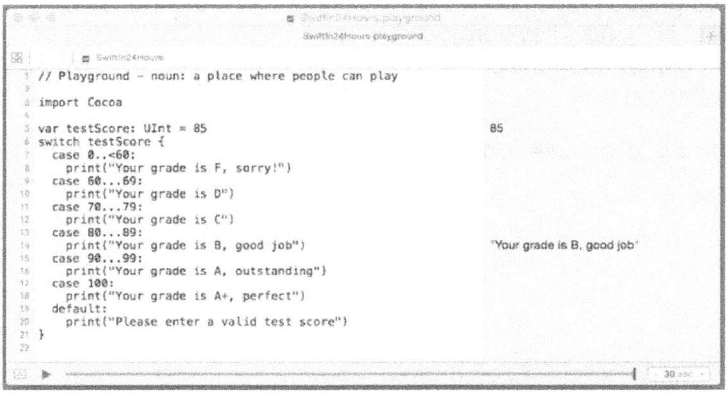

Figure 4-5. Using the Switch Statement With Interval Matching

With reference to Figure 4-5, the code has a `switch` statement with multiple cases, the majority of which include ranges for interval matching. Also note that the variable `testScore` is defined as an unsigned integer via the `UInt` type annotation; this insures that the input value is always a positive number. Change the variable to different values and verify the sidebar displays the correct text for each value.

The switch statement has additional functionality that makes it an even more powerful conditional construct; you'll learn about these a little later in this book.

Loops

The loop constructs execute a block of code zero or more times until a condition is met. Swift provides several types of `for` and `while` loops for this purpose.

For Loop

The `for` loop enables the repeated execution of a block of code until an optional Boolean condition evaluates to `false`. The syntax of the `for` loop is:

Listing 4-4. For Loop Statement

```
for initialization; conditional; increment {
    // Loop logic
}
```

The optional ***initialization*** expression can be of any type and is evaluated once. Here you typically initialize variables used during the loop logic and for expression evaluation. The optional Boolean ***conditional*** expression is evaluated before each iteration. If this expression evaluates to `true` the loop logic is executed. If the expression evaluates to `false` the loop logic is not executed and the loop statement is exited, with program execution continuing at the next statement. If a ***conditional*** expression is not provided it is considered `true`, and the loop logic is executed. In this scenario the loop logic would continue to be performed until a `break` or a `return` statement is executed. As shown above the body of the loop logic is enclosed in braces. After the code within the loop logic is executed the ***increment*** expression is evaluated, and execution returns to the conditional expression. The increment expression could change the value of the loop counter; change the value of a loop variable, etc.

For loops can be nested, enabling one loop to reside in another loop. Variables declared within the loop initialization expression are temporary and thus exist only within the body of loop.

Now let's develop an example; in your playground delete any existing code then add the following:

```
var sequence: UInt = 5
if (sequence >= 2) {
    var fn: UInt
    var fn1: UInt = 0
    var fn2: UInt = 1
    for var index:UInt=2; index<=sequence; index++ {
        fn = fn1 + fn2
        fn1 = fn2
        fn2 = fn
    }
```

}

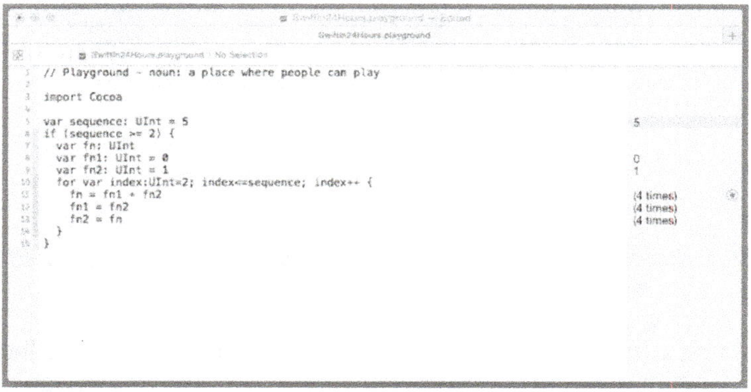

Figure 4-6. Using the For Loop

This code computes a sequence of Fibonacci numbers. As shown in Figure 4-6, the code includes a `for` loop with initialization, a conditional expression that controls the quantity of numbers computed, and a loop increment.

Note in the sidebar the expression **(4 times)** displayed across from each statement. This indicates the number loop iterations and hence the number of times the expression was computed. Now hover your mouse in the sidebar on the same line as the statement `fn = fn1 + fn2;` to the far right you'll see a *value history dot* (it looks like a dot). Tap this value history dot to open the playground **timeline**. The timeline enables you to see computed values for a line of code that's executed repeatedly, such as code inside a `for` or `while` loop. Figure 4-7 shows how the value computed for the statement `fn = fn1 + fn2` changes over time. The timeline also displays *console output,* e.g. output from your code's `print(_:)` statements.

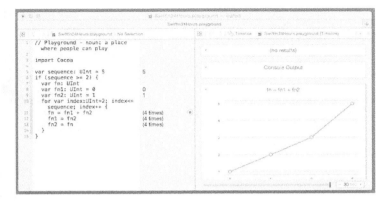

Figure 4-7. Displaying a For Loop Timeline

Change the variable `sequence` to different values and verify the timeline displays the correct Fibonacci sequence value.

For-in Loop

The `for-in` loop performs repeated execution of a block of code over a sequence, such as a range of numbers, items in a collection, or a collection of characters from a string. The syntax for the for-in loop is:

Listing 4-5. For-in Loop Statement

```
for varName in sequence {
  // Loop logic
}
```

The variable `varName` is set at the beginning of each loop iteration. The sequence can be a range of numbers defined using a Swift *range* operator, a Swift collection type instance, or the characters of a Swift string. The loop is executed as follows: the `for-in` variable is set to each sequence value and the loop logic (enclosed within braces) is executed accordingly.

Let's modify the previous example to use a `for-in` loop; in your playground update the `for` loop code you created previously with the following:

```
var sequence: UInt = 5
if (sequence >= 2) {
  var fn: UInt
  var fn1: UInt = 0
```

```
var fn2: UInt = 1

for _ in 2...sequence {

    fn = fn1 + fn2

    fn1 = fn2

    fn2 = fn

}

}
```

Figure 4-8. Using the For-In Loop

Let's review the changes shown in Figure 4-8. A `for-in` loop is used to execute the loop logic repetitively. The sequence of values is specified using the Swift closed-range (. . .) operator; in this case these range from 2 through the value of the variable `sequence`. As the loop variable is not used, you can ignore them by using an underscore (_) symbol in place of a loop variable name. In your playground change the variable `sequence` to different numbers and verify the timeline displays the computed values for the loop statement `fn = fn1 + fn2`.

While and Repeat-while Loops

Both the `while` loop and `repeat-while` loop perform repeated execution of a block of code while a Boolean condition evaluates to `true`. The difference between them is that the `while` loop condition is evaluated before each pass through the loop, and the `repeat-while` loop condition is evaluated at the end of each pass through the loop. The syntax for the `while` loop is:

Listing 4-6. While Loop Statement

```
while conditional {
```

```
  // Conditional logic
}
```

and the syntax for the `repeat-while` loop is:

```
repeat {
  // Conditional logic
} while conditional
```

The **conditional** expression is evaluated, if it evaluates to `true` the loop logic in the body of the `while` statement is executed, and the process is repeated. If the expression evaluates to `false`, the program exits the `while` statement and continues at the next statement. The program will also exit a `while` statement if a `break` or a `return` statement is executed within the loop body. Similar processing is performed for the `repeat-while` loop, the difference being that the conditional expression is evaluated after the loop logic is executed. Hence the `repeat-while` loop guarantees that the loop logic is executed at least once.

Now let's develop an example; in your playground delete any existing code then add the following:

```
var counter: UInt = 5
if (counter != 0) {
  while (counter > 0) {
    counter--
  }
  print("Blast-off!")
}
```

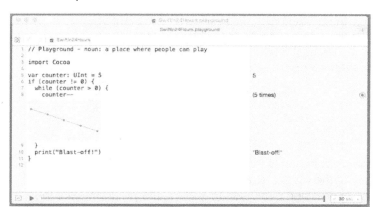

Figure 4-9. Using the While Loop

This code counts down to zero from its initial value and then prints a message to the console. As shown in Figure 4-9, the code includes a `while` loop with a conditional expression that controls the countdown until blast-off. Change the variable `counter` to different values and verify the timeline displays the change of the counter variable over time, and the console output displays the correct message.

So which loop should you use? The `for` loops are good for scenarios where you know ahead of time the number of loop iterations required. On the other hand, the `while` loops are preferred in scenarios where the number of loop iterations is not known in advance, and is determined during the body of the loop.

Control Transfer

The transfer-of-control constructs unconditionally cause a program to begin executing a different block of code. This enables you to change the order in which your code is executed.

Guard Statement

The `guard` statement, like the `if` statement, executes code depending on Boolean conditions. It differs from the `if` statement in that it is used to transfer control from the current enclosing scope if the condition evaluates to `false`, else it continues executing the code after the `guard` statement. The syntax for the `guard` statement is:

Listing 4-7. Guard Statement

```
guard Conditional expression 1 {
    // Control transfer statement(s) (false branch)
```

```
}
```

```
// Code following guard statement (true branch)
```

A guard statement can contain variable declarations (including optional binding); each variable/constant declared in an optional statement is available to the code following the statement (if it's conditional expression evaluates to true). The following code uses a guard statement to retrieve a value for an optional variable (using optional binding) named greeting and then prints the value if it exists:

```
guard let str = greeting {

   return

}

print(str)
```

Continue

The continue statement passes control to the next iteration of the nearest enclosing loop (for, while, repeat-while) statement in which it appears, bypassing any remaining statements in the loop statement body. The continue statement must appear within a loop statement. The following code illustrates use of the statement in a for loop that only displays odd numbers:

```
for (var ii=0; ii<maxNumber; ii++) {

   if (ii % 2) == 0 {

      continue

   }

   print(ii)

}
```

Break

The break statement terminates the execution of the nearest enclosing loop (for, while, repeat-while), or switch statement in which it appears. When used inside a loop statement, the program continues execution at the statement that follows the loop's closing brace (}). When used inside a switch statement, it causes the switch statement to end its execution immediately and transfer control to the first statement after the switch statement's closing brace.

Return

The `return` statement terminates execution of a method or function and returns control to the calling method/function. The `return` statement can also return a value to the calling method/function. The syntax for the `return` statement is:

```
return expression
```

The optional expression value is returned to the calling method/function and is converted to the type returned by the method/function.

Chapter **5**

STANDARD LIBRARY

The Swift programming language includes a Standard Library of built-in *Application Programming Interfaces* (APIs) that consist of a collection of data types, functions, and other tools. In this chapter you will learn about some of the more commonly used Standard Library APIs.

Swift has two categories of types: *named types* that are given a name when defined, and *compound types* that are unnamed and defined in the language itself. Named types have properties and methods, and you can extend them to add additional data and functionality. Included amongst the Swift Standard Library named types are numeric types, strings and characters, and collections types, which you will learn about next.

Numeric Types

Swift defines a number of numeric types that can be used to represent integers and real numbers of various sizes. The numeric types are *value types;* this means that instances of these types are copied when passed as arguments to functions or methods, or when assigned to a variable. The following paragraphs provide an overview of the Swift numeric types; you should refer to the Swift **Standard Library Reference** for additional documentation on these APIs.

Integers

Swift provides both signed and unsigned integer data types. The basic Swift signed integer type, `Int`, has the same size as your hardware platform's native word size. For example, on a 32-bit platform an `Int` is 32 bits in length, whereas on a 64-bit platform it is 64 bits in length. To define an integer of a specific size, Swift provides the following types:

`Int8` – an 8-bit integer

`Int16` – a 16-bit integer

`Int32` – a 32-bit integer

`Int64` – a 64-bit integer

Swift also provides several unsigned integer data types for unsigned values:

`UInt` – unsigned integer with the same size as the platform's native word size

`UInt8` – an 8-bit unsigned integer

`UInt16` – a 16-bit unsigned integer

`UInt32` – a 32-bit unsigned integer

`UInt64` – a 64-bit unsigned integer

Each type has `min` and `max` properties that can be used to retrieve the minimum and maximum value for the corresponding integer type. For example the minimum value for a basic integer would be retrieved using the `min` property of the `Int` type.

```
Int.min
```

Integer literals can be written in code using several different numeral systems: 1) decimal number system, 2) binary number with the `0b` prefix, 3) octal number with the `0o` prefix, or hexadecimal number with the `0x` prefix. The following statements provide several different ways of coding the decimal value of 21 as an integer literal:

```
21              // 21 in decimal notation

0b00010101   // 21 in binary notation

0o025          // 21 in octal notation

0x15           // 21 in hexadecimal notation
```

Real Numbers

Swift represents real numbers as floating-point values with the `Float` and `Double` types. The `Float` type represents a 32-bit single precision floating-point number, while the `Double` type represents a 64-bit double precision floating-point number.

Floating-point literals can be written with decimal or hexadecimal notation. They must be written with a number on both sides of the decimal point (e.g. `0.5` not `.5`). Floating-point literals can also have an optional exponent, indicated by a lower/uppercase `e` for decimal floating-point values, or a lower/uppercase `p` for hexadecimal floating-point values. The following are valid floating-point literal numbers:

```
1.5            // 1.5
```

`-1.5e3`	*// means -1.5 x 10exp3 = -1.5 x 1000*
`3.1415e-1`	*// means 3.1415 x 10exp-1 = 3.1415 x 0.1*
`0x10p4`	*// means 16 x 2exp4 = 16 x 16*
`-0xCp-2`	*// means -12 x 2exp-2 = -12 x 0.25*

Booleans

Swift defines a Boolean type, a data type that can only have two possible values: **true** or **false**. These two values are represented by the Swift Boolean literal values `true` and `false`. The keyword `Bool` is used to define a Boolean data type, as shown in the following example:

```
var isMonday: Bool
```

As you have already seen in numerous examples, Boolean values are often used with conditional statements such as `if` statements and `for` loops.

Strings and Characters

Swift provides the standard library `String` type for working with text strings, an ordered collection of Unicode-compliant characters. In fact, a Swift `String` is actually a collection of Swift `Character` values arranged in a specified order. These are value types and hence are copied on assignment or when passed as an argument or a return value. The following paragraphs provide an overview of the `String` type; you should refer to the **Swift Standard Library** Reference for additional documentation on this API.

String Literals

Earlier in this book you learned how to create a string literal by enclosing text within double quotes. You can also use create a string instance using Swift *initializer syntax*. The following example creates a `String` instance as a string literal and assigns that instance to a variable named `greeting`.

```
var greeting = "Hello, World!"
```

String Initializers

A Swift String is implemented as a Swift *structure* (don't worry if you're not familiar with structures, we'll be covering them in an upcoming chapter); as such Swift *initializer syntax* can be used to create and initialize new String instances. This syntax requires that you type the `String` keyword followed by a string argument within parentheses. The argument can be a string literal or any expression that evaluates to a string. The following example creates a `String` instance using initializer syntax and assigns that instance to a variable named `greeting`.

```
var greeting = String("Hello, World!")
```

String Concatenation

The addition (+) operator can be used to chain two strings together to create a new `String` value. The following code concatenates two string literals, creating a new `String` value that is assigned to the variable greeting.

```
var greeting = "Hello, " + "World!"
```

The addition assignment operator (+=) can also be used to combine string concatenation and assignment in a single statement. The following code uses this operator to concatenate the variable `greeting` with another `String` instance.

```
var greeting = "Hello"

greeting += ", World!"
```

You can also append `String` or `Character` values to an existing string instance with the String `append(_:)` method. The following example uses this method to append a string to the variable `greeting`.

```
var greeting = "Hello"

greeting.append(", World!")
```

String Interpolation

Swift also provides a *string interpolation* mechanism that enables you to insert the value of an expression within a string literal. The expression can be made up of existing variables, literals, and/or expressions. Each value that you insert into a string literal via interpolation is enclosed within parentheses and preceded by a backslash.

Now let's demonstrate the use of string interpolation with an example; in your playground delete any existing code then add the following:

```
var magicNumber = 21

"Your magic number today is \(magicNumber)"
```

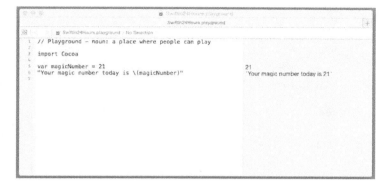

Figure 5-1. String Interpolation

The code shown in Figure 5-1 prints a string literal and uses string interpolation to include the value of the variable `magicNumber` in the literal. Change the variable to different values and verify the sidebar displays the correct text for each value.

Characters

A Swift `Character` type is a single, Unicode-compliant text character. As mentioned earlier a `String` is actually a collection of `Character` values. A Character can be created as a single character string literal by surrounding it with double-quotes, for example the following code defines a variable named `exclamationPoint` of type `Character`:

```
var exclamationPoint: Character = "!"
```

The addition (+) and addition assignment (+=) operators can be used to add a single character to a string to create a new `String` value. The following example concatenates the variable above to a String literal named `greeting`:

```
var greeting = "Hello, World"

greeting += exclamationPoint
```

You can also append a `Character` to an existing `String` using the `String` type's `append( :)` method.

The `characters` property of a `String` returns a collection of `Characters` that can be iterated over with a `for-in` loop. OK, so now let's demonstrate use of a collection of character values with an example. In your playground delete any existing code then add the following:

```
for char in "Hello, World!".characters {
```

```
    print(char)

}
```

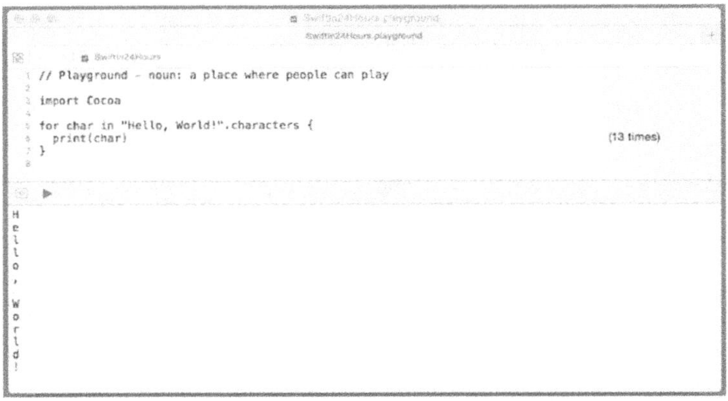

Figure 5-2. Using Character Values

In Chapter 4 you learned that the Swift `for-in` loop could be used over a collection of `Characters` values. The code shown in Figure 5-2 demonstrates this; it creates a string literal and then uses the `characters` property to retrieve a collection of characters from the string and use a `for-in` loop to print each character. You should change the string literal to different values and verify the sidebar displays each corresponding character value appropriately.

Bridging with NSString

Swift provides a variety of mechanisms that enable you to use the Cocoa and Cocoa Touch APIs in your Swift code. One such mechanism, *String bridging,* automatically bridges between the `String` and `NSString` types. `NSString` is the Foundation Framework API for creating and managing text strings. String bridging augments the capabilities of the Swift `String` type by extending the `NSString` properties and methods to `String` instances. To use string bridging in Swift code you simply import the Foundation Framework API. Let's demonstrate string bridging in your playground; delete any existing code then add the following:

```
import Cocoa

let greeting = "hello, world!"

print(greeting.capitalizedString)

print(greeting.uppercaseString)

if greeting.lowercaseString.hasPrefix("hello") {
```

```
print("Begins with a greeting!")
}
```

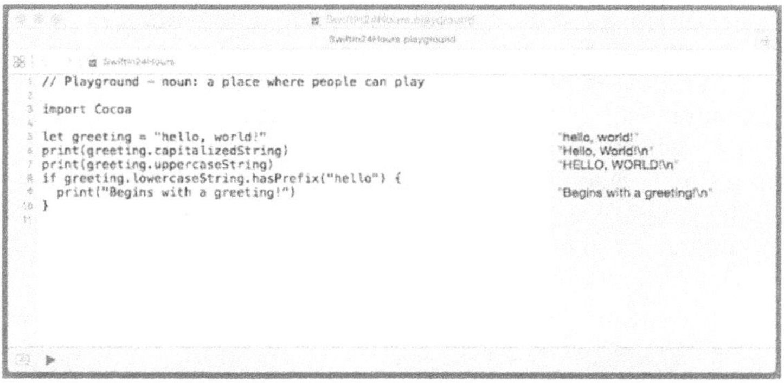

Figure 5-3. String Bridging

The `import Cocoa` statement imports the Cocoa API; this includes the Foundation Framework API. As `String` instances are automatically bridged to the `NSString` type, you can access the `NSString` APIs; in this case the `capitalizedString` and `uppercaseString` properties as well as the `hasPrefix` method. As shown in Figure 5-3, the code displays the capitalized and upper-case versions of the greeting string, and also checks to see whether the string begins with an appropriate greeting. Change the value for the variable and observe the output in the sidebar.

Collections

A collection groups a variable number of data elements into a single unit. Swift programming language provides APIs for three collection types – arrays, sets, and dictionaries. An array is an ordered collection of values, each identified by an index, which may include duplicates. A set is an unordered collection of distinct values. A dictionary is an unordered collection of key-value pairs, such that each key appears at most once in the collection. The collection types are *value types;* as such instances of these types are copied when passed as arguments to functions or methods, or when assigned to a variable. A collection instance created as a constant (via the `let` keyword) it is read-only, whereas one created as a variable is read/write – i.e. its elements and number can be changed. The following paragraphs provide an overview of the collections types; you should refer to the Swift **Standard Library Reference** for the complete documentation on these APIs.

Arrays

The Swift `Array` type enables you to create a collection of data elements (i.e. values) of the same type in an ordered list. Array elements are selected by indices, and these indices can be computed at run time. In addition, an array can have duplicate values, each of which appears at a different position in the list. The syntax for notating the type of an array is `Array<DataType>` where `DataType` is the type of the data elements contained in the array. You can also declare the type of an array with the shorthand notation `[DataType]`. The following example declares an array of `String` instances and assigns the array to a variable named `colors`:

```
var colors: Array<String>
```

With shorthand notation the declaration changes to:

```
var colors: [String]
```

Each array element can be access via a corresponding key, or *index*, a positive integer value. The Swift `Array` type is *zero-based,* meaning that the minimum valid value for any array index is zero. Swift also performs bounds checking on every array access to verify that your code is not trying to access a value outside of the size of the array. The `Array` type includes several mechanisms for creating and accessing arrays, and also a variety of methods for manipulating array instances. You'll learn about these next.

Creating Arrays

Similar to the `String` type, the Swift `Array` type is implemented as a structure; as such Swift *initializer syntax* can be used to create and initialize new `Array` instances. Swift also provides literal notation for array creation and assignment.

Swift provides several array initializers that enable you to create an array with zero or more values. The syntax for creating an empty array using array initializer syntax is:

```
[DataType]()
```

The following example creates an empty array that can hold String instances and assigns it to a variable named `colors`:

```
var colors = [String]()
```

The `Array` type also includes an initializer for creating an array instance of a specified size with all of its elements set to a specified default value. The syntax for this array initializer is:

```
[DataType](count: size, repeatedValue: defaultValue)
```

The values for `size` and `defaultValue` are arguments to the initializer, where `size` is of type `Int` and `defaultValue` is the type specified for the data elements. The following example creates an array that holds three integers, each initialized to the value 10, and assigns the array to a variable named `luckyNumbers`:

```
var luckyNumbers = [Int](count: 3, repeatedValue: 10)
```

Swift array literal notation can also be used for creating `Array` instances. You code an array literal as a list of values, separated by commas, all surrounded by a pair of square brackets. The following example declares an array literal of `String` values assigned to a variable named `colors`:

```
var colors = ["red", "green", "blue"]
```

Once you have created an Array instance you can append more values to it using the `Array` type's `append(_:)` method. The following code adds another color to the `colors` array declared above using the `append(_:)` method:

```
colors.append("yellow")
```

Additional methods are provided to insert and remove elements for an array instance.

Accessing Array Elements

The `Array` type includes a subscript syntax for accessing or modifying an array. You can retrieve a value from an array instance by supplying the index of the value within square brackets immediately after the instance name. The following code access the first value of the `colors` array and assigns it to the variable `favoriteColor`:

```
var favoriteColor = colors[0]
```

You can use subscript syntax to modify the value of an array element via assignment. The following example changes the first element of the `colors` array to the value `orange`:

```
colors[0] = "orange"
```

Array subscript syntax can also be used to modify a range of array elements with the `range` operator. You can get a subset of existing elements in an array as a new array, or set a subset of existing elements in an array to new values. The range is specified by using the closed range operator (`...`); this defines the range of elements within square brackets immediately after the instance name. The following code retrieves the first three elements of the `colors` array and assigns this to a new array named `favoriteColors`:

```
var favoriteColors = colors[0...2]
```

You can also modify a range of values at once, setting them to new values and even decreasing the number of values. The following example modifies the `colors` array, both changing the length of the array by replacing elements 1 through 3 (i.e. 3 elements) with 2 elements and setting those to new values:

```
colors[1...3] = ["green", "gold"]
```

As a result of this operation, the `colors` array has been reduced in size from four to three elements.

Iterating Over an Array

You can iterate over the elements of an array with a `for-in` loop. The following code prints each of the values of the `colors` array:

```
for color in colors {
    print(color)
}
```

Now let's demonstrate our use of arrays with an example; in your playground delete any existing code then add the following:

```
var colors = [String]()
colors.append("red")
colors.append("green")
colors.insert("blue", atIndex:1)
colors.append("orange")
colors[1...3] = ["yellow", "violet"]
colors[2] = "gray"
for color in colors {
    print("This color is \(color)")
}
```

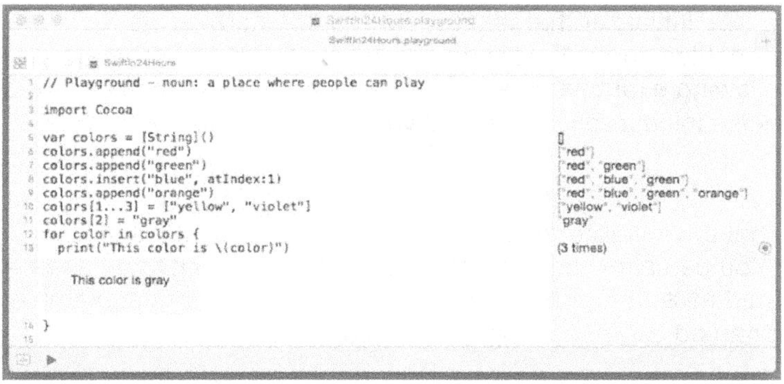

Figure 5-4. Swift Arrays

The code demonstrates use of various `Array` type APIs. The code shown
above and in Figure 5-4 first creates an empty array of type `String`
assigned to the variable `colors`. It then uses the String `append(_:)`
method to add several String instances to the array. Next the String
`insert(_:atIndex:)` method is used to insert a new `String` instance
to the array between the existing instances. Subscript syntax is used to
modify the array, changing both its size and several of its elements.
Subscript syntax is also used to access and modify an array element.
Finally a `for-in` loop is used to iterate over the array. You should
experiment with this code (e.g. adding more colors, changing their values,
etc.) and observe the output in the sidebar.

Sets

The Swift `Set` type enables you to create an unordered collection of
distinct data elements, each of the same type. The syntax for notating the
type of a set is `Set<DataType>` where `DataType` is the type of the data
elements contained in the set. Each element of a `Set` instance must be
hashable (i.e. unique).

Creating Sets

Swift *initializer syntax* can be used to create and initialize new `Set`
instances. The syntax for creating an empty set using `Set` initializer
syntax is:

```
Set[DataType]()
```

The following example creates an empty set that can hold `String`
instances and assigns it to a variable named `colors`:

```
var colors = Set[String]()
```

There is also a `Set` initializer that takes a Swift array literal as its argument; this enables you to create a set initialized with a number of values. The following example creates a set named `colors` that can hold `String` instances, initialized with several values:

```
var colors = Set(["red", "green", "blue"])
```

Notice above that the initializer includes an array literal of values inside parentheses. You can also code an array literal and assign it to a variable explicitly declared as a `Set`. The following modifies the previous example to create a set named `colors` assigned to an array literal of `String` values:

```
var colors:Set = ["red", "green", "blue"]
```

The `count` property returns a positive integer value of the number of elements in the set. The following code gets the number of values in the `colors` set and assigns this value to the variable `numberOfColors`:

```
var numberOfColors = colors.count
```

Adding and Removing Set Elements

The `Set` type includes APIs for adding and removing elements. You can add a new element to a `Set` instance using the `insert(_:)` method; the value being added must not be a duplicate of a value that already is present in the set. The following code adds a new value to the `colors` set:

```
colors.insert("yellow")
```

The `remove(_:)` method removes an element from a set where the argument to the method is the element in the set to be removed. This method returns an optional of the type stored in the Set – if the optional is `nil` then the value was not present in the set and thus not removed, otherwise the returned optional contains the value removed. The following removes a value from the `colors` set and stores the returned value as the optional `removedColor`:

```
var removedColor = colors.remove("yellow")
```

The `subtract(_:)` method removes the values of the input set/array from the current set, returning a new set. The `removeAll(keepCapacity:)` method can be used to remove all of the elements of the specified set.

Checking for Membership in Sets

The `Set` type includes APIs for checking if a set contains an element or collection of elements (i.e. the elements of another `Set` or `Array` instance). The `contains(_:)` method takes a single element as an argument and returns `true` if the set contains the specified argument. The following returns `true` if the `colors` array contains the value `blue`:

```
var containsBlue = colors.contains("blue")
```

The `isSubsetOf(_:)` method takes a `Set` or `Array` instance as an argument and returns `true` if every element in the set is within the input set/array. The following creates a set of two values assigned to the variable `twoColors` and then uses the `isSubsetOf(_:)` method to determine if its values are within the `colors` set:

```
var twoColors: Set = ["red", "blue"]

var isSubset = twoColors.isSubsetOf(colors)
```

Conversely, the `isSupersetOf(_:)` method takes a `Set` or `Array` instance as an argument and returns `true` if the set contains every element within the input set/array. The following code returns `true` if the `colors` method is a superset of the `twoColors` set:

```
var isSuperset = colors.isSupersetOf(twoColors)
```

Additional APIs are provided for performing set operations (e.g. union, intersection, exclusive or, etc.).

Iterating Over a Set

You can iterate over the elements of a set with a `for-in` loop, similar to an array. Now let's demonstrate our use of sets with an example; in your playground delete any existing code then add the following:

```
var colors = Set(["red", "green", "blue"])

colors.insert("orange")

var numberOfColors = colors.count

colors.contains("blue")

var twoColors: Set = ["red", "blue"]

twoColors.isSubsetOf(colors)

colors.isSupersetOf(twoColors)

var newColors = colors.subtract(twoColors)

var duplicateColors = twoColors.union(newColors)

for color in duplicateColors {
```

```
print("\(color)")
```

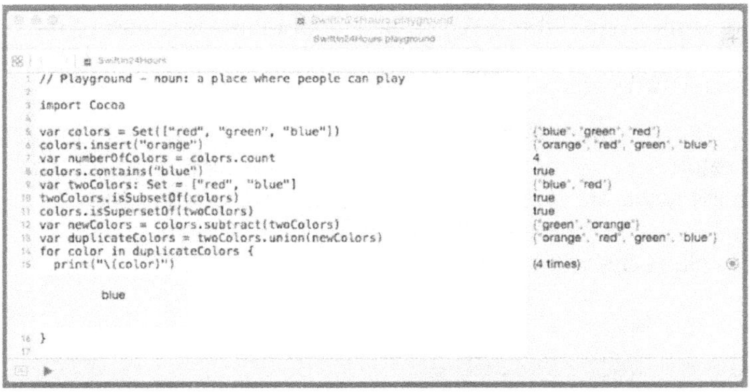

}

Figure 5-5. Swift Sets

The code listed in Figure 5-5 demonstrates use of various `Set` type APIs. It first creates a set of `String` instances assigned to the variable `colors`. The code then uses the String `insert(_:)` method to add a String instance to the array. Next a new set is created using a `Set` initializer and the relationship between the two sets is tested using the `isSubsetOf(_:)` and `isSuperSetOf(_:)` methods. Another set is then created as a subset of the original via the `subtract(_:)` method. The `union(_:)` method is used to create a new set composed of all the values of two existing sets. Finally a `for-in` loop is used to iterate over the set. You should experiment with this code (e.g. adding more colors, changing their values, etc.) and observe the output in the sidebar.

Dictionaries

The Swift `Dictionary` type enables you to create an unordered collection of key-value pairs. The dictionary keys must be of the same type and the corresponding values must be of a single type. In addition the keys must be hashable, thereby guaranteeing that each key appears at most once in a dictionary instance. Dictionary elements are selected by key, and each key can be set or computed at run time. The syntax for notating the type of a Dictionary is `Dictionary<KeyType,` `ValueType>` where `KeyType` is the type of the keys and `ValueType` that of the corresponding values. You can also declare the type of a dictionary with the shorthand notation `[KeyType: ValueType]`. The following example declares a dictionary of `String:Integer` instances and assigns the dictionary to a variable named `rgb`:

```
var rgb: Dictionary<String, Int>
```

With shorthand notation the declaration changes to:

```
var rgb: [String, Int]
```

The `Dictionary` type includes several mechanisms for creating and accessing dictionaries, and also a variety of methods for manipulating dictionary instances. You'll learn about these next.

Creating Dictionaries

Swift *initializer syntax* can be used to create and initialize new `Dictionary` instances. Swift also provides literal notation for dictionary creation and assignment.

Swift provides several array initializers that enable you to create an array with zero or more values. The syntax for creating an empty dictionary using initializer syntax is:

```
[KeyType: ValueType]()
```

The following example creates an empty dictionary that holds RGB codes of color names and assigns it to a variable named `rgb`:

```
var rgb = [String: Int]()
```

If the type of a Dictionary is already known, you can create an empty dictionary with the empty dictionary literal, written as `[:]`. The following code modifies the previous example to create the empty `rgb` Dictionary instance:

```
var rgb: [String: Int] = [:]
```

Swift literal notation can also be used for creating `Dictionary` instances. You code a dictionary literal as a list of `key:value` pairs, separated by commas, all surrounded by a pair of square brackets. The following example declares an dictionary literal of `String:Int` values assigned to the variable named `rgb`:

```
var rgb = ["red":0xFF0000, "blue":0x0000FF]
```

The `Dictionary` read-only `count` property can be used to check the number of items in a dictionary; the Boolean `isEmpty` property can be used to check whether there are any items in a dictionary.

Accessing and Modifying Dictionaries Elements

The `Dictionary` type includes subscript syntax for accessing or modifying its elements. You can retrieve a value from a dictionary instance by supplying the key of the value within square brackets immediately after the instance name. This returns an optional with an underlying type of the dictionary's value; if the dictionary does not contain a value for the corresponding key it returns `nil`. The following code access the value associated with the key "red" of the `rgb` dictionary instance and assigns it to the variable `redCode`:

```
var redCode = rgb["red"]
```

You can also use subscript syntax to add a new dictionary element or modify an existing element's value. The following example adds a new item to the `rgb` dictionary:

```
rgb["green"] = 0x00FF00
```

Subscript syntax can also be used to remove an item from a dictionary by assigning a value of `nil` for that key.

As an alternative to subscript syntax, the `Dictionary` type includes an API, `updateValue(_:forKey:)`, that can be used to set or update the value for a specific key. The method returns an optional value of the dictionary's value type; if no value existed prior to the update it returns `nil`, otherwise it returns the old value. The following example uses this API to add an item to the `rgb` dictionary:

```
var oldValue = rgb.updateValue(0x00FF00,
forKey:"green")
```

The `removeAll(keepCapacity:)` method can be used to remove all the items from a dictionary.

Iterating Over a Dictionary

You can iterate over the elements of a dictionary with a `for-in` loop. Each item in the dictionary is returned as a `(key, value)` **tuple**; in the next chapter you'll learn about tuples. The following code prints each color and corresponding value of the `rgb` dictionary:

```
for (color, value) in rgb {
   print("\(color) value is \(value)")
}
```

The `Dictionary` type also includes two properties for iterating over a dictionary's keys and values. The read-only `keys` property returns a collection of all the dictionary's keys. The `values` property returns a collection of all the dictionary's values. The elements from each of these collections are typically accessed using a `for-in` loop.

Now let's demonstrate our use of dictionaries with an example; in your playground delete any existing code then add the following:

```
var rgb = ["red":0xFF0000, "green":0x00FF00]

rgb["blue"] = 0x0000FF

var oldValue = rgb.updateValue(0xFFFF00,
forKey:"yellow")

for (color, value) in rgb {

  print("\(color) value is \(value)")

}

let colors = rgb.keys

for color in colors {

  print(color)

}
```

Figure 5-6. Swift Dictionaries

The code shown above and in Figure 5-6 demonstrates use of various `Dictionary` type APIs. It first creates a dictionary of `String:Int` items using a dictionary literal and assign this to the variable `rgb`. It then uses subscripting to add an RGB code for the color `blue`. Next it uses the `updateValue(_:forKey:)` method to add an RGB code for the color `yellow`. A `for-in` loop is used to iterate over the `rgb` dictionary, printing the color and corresponding RGB code. Finally a collection of all the keys of the `rgb` dictionary is retrieved using the `keys` property and then printed using a `for-in` loop. You should experiment with this code (e.g. adding more `color:value` pairs, changing colors/values, etc.) and observe the output in the sidebar.

Functions

The Swift Standard Library defines numerous built-in functions that you can use to perform common programming tasks. In this paragraph you'll learn about several of commonly used Standard Library functions. You should refer to the Swift **Standard Library Reference** for additional documentation on the built-in functions.

Printing

The `print(_:separator:terminator:)` function writes the item arguments to the standard output. The syntax of the function is:

```
print(_ items: T, separator: String, terminator:
String)
```

The `items` are of type `T`, and must conform to either the `Streamable`, `CustomStringConvertible`, or `CustomDebugStreamConvertible` protocol. Types that conform to these protocols must have a textual representation. The Standard Library has numerous types (e.g. `String`, `Int`, `Float`, etc.) that conform to these protocols. The `separator` argument separates each item, and the `terminator` ends the output. Both the `separator` and `terminator` have default values such that if neither is provided the function will print a single `item` argument to the console, terminated with a newline. If a newline is not desired the `terminator` argument should be empty quotes (`""`).

The following example creates a String literal and then prints it to the standard output with a trailing newline:

```
var greeting = "Hello, World!"

print(greeting)
```

The next example creates two String literals and prints them to the standard output, each separated by a comma, with a trailing newline:

```
var greeting = "Hello, World!"
var goodbye = "Goodbye"

print(greeting, goodbye, separator: ", ")
```

Algorithms

The `sort(_:)` function performs an in-place sort of its argument, a Swift `Array` instance. The syntax for the `sort(_:)` function is:

```
sort(arg: Array<T>)
```

The type of the `Array` elements must conform to the Swift `Comparable` protocol; this means that it must be possible to compare the values of the `Array` elements using the Swift `<`, `>`, `<=`, and `>=` operators. Now earlier you learned that Swift arrays are passed by value, meaning a copy of the `Array` instance is passed to functions but the original instance is unchanged. As the `sort(_:)` function performs an in-place sort of its (array) argument, a *reference* (i.e. pointer) to the function must be passed. This is accomplished by using a Swift *in-out* parameter (specified in a parameter definition with the `inout` keyword); this is indicated in the function argument by placing an ampersand (`&`) immediately prior to the array instance. The following example creates an `Array` instance named `testScores` and then sorts its elements using this function:

```
var testScores = [75, 90, 78, 95, 85]

sort(&testScores)
```

The `sorted(_:)` function performs a sort of the input argument, a Swift `Array` instance, and returns a new sorted array, leaving the input unmodified. As this method does not modify the argument of the `sort(_:)` function, the instance is supplied directly (i.e. the `inout` operator is not required). The following example creates an `Array` instance and then returns a sorted instance in a new variable named `sortedScores`:

```
var testScores = [75, 90, 78, 95, 85]

var sortedScores = sorted(testScores)
```

The `find(_:)` function returns the first index where over the *domain* (argument 1) the input *value* (argument 2) is found, or returns `nil` if the value is not found. The syntax for the function is:

```
var index: Int? = find(domain: C, value: Element)
```

The `domain` argument is of type `C`, meaning that this argument must conform to the Swift `CollectionType` protocol. Corresponding types include the Standard Library collection types, the `String` type, and ranges created with the Swift range operators. The `value` argument must conform to the `Equatable` protocol, meaning that instances of this type can be compared for value equality using the operators `==` and `!=`. The following example returns the first index of a test score whose value is 95:

```
var gradeA = find(domain: [75, 90, 78, 95, 85], value: 95)
```

The `abs(_:)` function returns the absolute value of the input numeric argument. The following example returns the absolute value of its input argument:

```
var absProduct = abs(-4.2 * 17.6)
```

General

The `assert(_:_:file:line:)` function performs an *assertion,* constructs commonly placed in your code to check the existence of a condition. The syntax for the `assert(_:_:file:line:)` function is:

```
assert(_ condition: Bool, _ message: String, file file:
StaticString = default, line line: UWord = default)
```

The condition argument is an expression that evaluates to a `Boolean`. If the condition evaluates to `true` your code continues executing as usual, but if it evaluates to `false` the optional message is displayed, code execution ends, and your app is terminated.

Protocols

The Swift Standard Library defines an extensive collection of *protocols* that you can use to perform common programming tasks. Briefly, a protocol defines a specification in the form of methods, properties, and other requirements that can be implemented by conforming types. In the Protocols section of Chapter 9 you'll learn what protocols are and how to create and use them. A few of the most commonly used Standard Library protocols are introduced below. You should refer to the Swift **Standard Library Reference** for documentation on the Standard Library protocols and how to use them.

The `CustomStringConvertible` protocol specifies requirements for a type that provides a customized textual representation. This is commonly used to write custom values of conforming types to an output stream, using the Standard Library `print(_:)` function or some other mechanism. The protocol declares a single read-only instance property named `description` of type `String`.

The `Equatable` protocol specifies requirements for conforming types that can be compared to one another for value equality. The protocol declares functions for the operators `==` and `!=`.

The `Hashable` protocol specifies requirements for a type that can be converted to a hash value for use as a Dictionary key. The protocol declares a single read-only instance property named `hashValue` of type `Int`.

The `Comparable` protocol specifies requirements for types that can be compared using the Swift relational operators. The protocol declares functions for the operators <, <=, >, and >=.

The `BooleanType` protocol specifies requirements for a type that represents a Boolean value. The protocol declares a single read-only instance property named `boolValue`.

The `GeneratorType` protocol specifies requirements for a type that can be used for iteration over a Swift sequence, where a sequence can be a range of numbers defined using a Swift *range* operator, a Swift collection type instance, or the characters of a Swift string. The protocol declares the *associated type* `Element` (defined as the type of the elements of the sequence) and the instance method `next()` that returns the next element in the sequence (or `nil` if no next element exists).

Chapter 6

TUPLES

In mathematics, a *tuple* is an ordered list of 0 or more elements, which is usually written by listing the elements within parentheses with each element separated by a comma. They are commonly used to describe mathematical objects such as complex numbers, vectors, etc. In computer science, tuples provide a similar abstraction, i.e. they are used to represent a grouping of elements as a single compound type.

Swift provides a tuple type similar to the mathematical concept. The elements within a tuple can be of any type, including other tuples. In Swift tuples are commonly used to create and pass around temporary groups of related values. They are often used to provide return values for functions; this enables you to code functions that return more information (i.e. values) without having to wrap all of this information in a single named type.

Creating Tuples

A Swift tuple is notated as an unnamed, ordered, comma-separated list of zero or more values enclosed within parentheses. The elements of a tuple can be of any type, including other tuples. The following code creates a two-element tuple that is assigned to a variable named `rgbColor`:

```
var rgbColor = ("red", 0xFF0000)
```

You can also name the individual elements of a tuple when defined by preceding the value of each element with an identifier. The following creates the `rgbColor` tuple and also names its individual elements:

```
var rgbColor = (color: "red", value: 0xFF0000)
```

You can access a tuple's individual elements using its element names (if provided) or by using index numbers starting at zero. The following example demonstrates the two methods of accessing the first element of the tuple `rgbColor`:

```
var color = rgbColor.0

var color = rgbColor.color
```

You can also assign values to the elements of a tuple using element names or index numbers. Now let's demonstrate creation and use of tuples with an example; in your playground delete any existing code then

67

add the following:

```
var rgbColor = (color:"red", code:0xFF0000)
print("The rgb color is \(rgbColor.color)")
print("The rgb code is \(rgbColor.code)")
rgbColor.color = "blue"
rgbColor.code = 0x0000FF
print("The rgb code for \(rgbColor.color) is
\(rgbColor.code)")
```

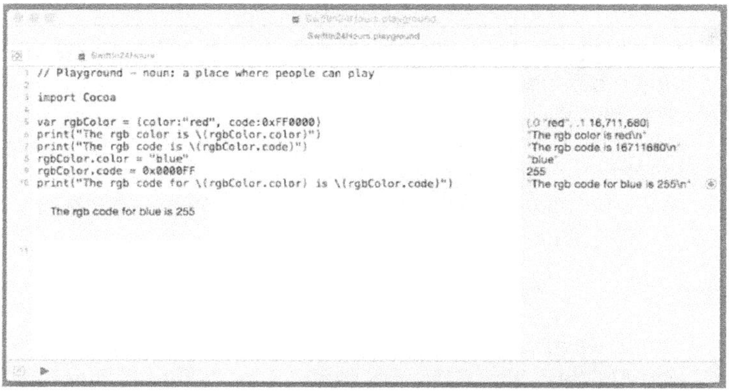

Figure 6-1. Creating Tuples

This code demonstrates creation and use of tuples. As depicted in Figure 6-1 it first creates a tuple of type `(String, Int)` and assigns it to the variable `rgbColor`. Next it prints out the individual values of the tuple. Finally it sets values for each of the tuple's elements and prints out these values. You should experiment with this code (e.g. changing colors/codes, etc.) and observe the output in the sidebar.

Tuples with Switch Statements

Tuples can be used with `switch` statements to test multiple values within one or more `switch` cases. Each element of a tuple can be tested, and you can use the underscore symbol (_) to indicate a discarded value (i.e., a value in the tuple that is not tested). Let's demonstrate this with an example; in your playground delete any existing code and add the following:

```
var testScore = ("A", 93)
switch (testScore) {
```

```
case ("A", _):
  print("Your GPA is 4.0")
case ("B", _):
  print("Your GPA is 3.0")
case ("C", _):
  print("Your GPA is 2.0")
case ("D", _):
  print("Your GPA is 1.0")
case ("F", _):
  print("Your GPA is 0.0")
default:
  print("Invalid letter grade")
}
```

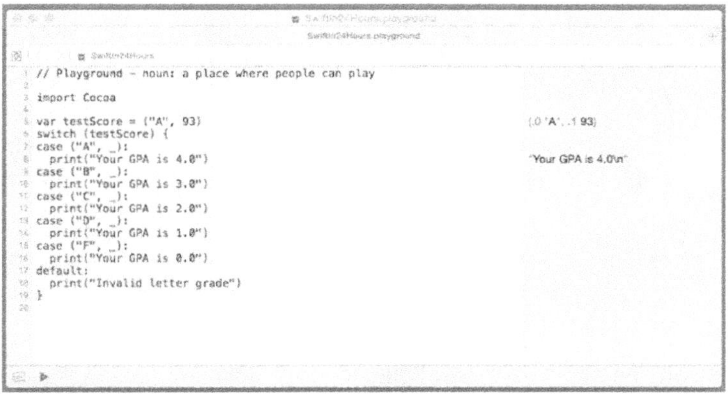

Figure 6-2. Using Tuples with Switch Statements

The following code demonstrates how a tuple can be used with a `switch` statement to test grades and print out a Grade Point Average (GPA). Referring to Figure 6-2 it creates a two-element tuple assigned to the variable `testScore`, and then uses a `switch` statement to test the letter grade for each score, returning a corresponding GPA. Note that the underscore symbol is used to discard the percentage grade and only test the letter grade for computing the GPA. You should experiment with this code, providing different letter grades and test scores, and observe the output in the sidebar.

You can also use value binding for `switch` cases, thereby enabling you to set a value for a variable. You bind a value to a constant using the `let` keyword; whereas you bind a value to a variable using the `var` keyword. Earlier in the chapter on Optionals you learned how to bind a value to a constant/variable within an `if` statement. Value binding is also commonly used with tuples to set the value of one or more of the elements in a `switch` case. The syntax for value binding of a tuple element within a switch case is:

```
var switchVar = (value1, value2)
switch (switchVar) {
   case (value1, let varName):
   // Case logic
}
```

As shown above, a two-element tuple is created and assigned to the variable `switchVar`. A switch statement then tests the variable; if the first element of the case tuple matches the first element of `switchVar` it binds the constant `varName` to the second element of the tuple (`value2`), which can then be used within the body of the corresponding case. Now let's demonstrate value binding with `switch` cases; in your playground delete any existing code and add the following:

```
var grade = (95, "Excellent work")
switch (grade) {
   case (90...99, let comment):
     print("You earned an A, \(comment)")
   case (80...89, let comment):
     print("You earned a B, \(comment)")
   // Code for additional cases (see Figure 6-3)
}
```

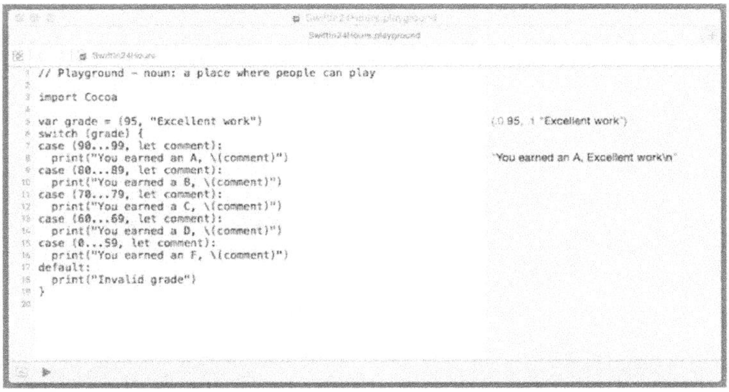

```
// Playground - noun: a place where people can play

import Cocoa

var grade = (95, "Excellent work")                    (0 95, 1 "Excellent work")
switch (grade) {
case (90...99, let comment):
    print("You earned an A, \(comment)")              "You earned an A, Excellent work\n"
case (80...89, let comment):
    print("You earned a B, \(comment)")
case (70...79, let comment):
    print("You earned a C, \(comment)")
case (60...69, let comment):
    print("You earned a D, \(comment)")
case (0...59, let comment):
    print("You earned an F, \(comment)")
default:
    print("Invalid grade")
}
```

Figure 6-3. Value Binding of Tuples with Switch Statements

The code of Figure 6-3 demonstrates value binding of tuples with `switch` statements. It first creates a tuple of type `(Int, String)` and assigns it to the variable `grade`. Next a switch statement tests `grade`; in each `case` it binds the second element of the case tuple (the constant `comment`) to the second element of `grade`. If the `case` matches (i.e. the first element of `grade` matches the first element of the `case` tuple) it prints out the letter grade along with the value of `comment`. You should experiment with this code (e.g. changing the score and the corresponding comment) and observe the output in the sidebar.

Chapter 7

FUNCTIONS

Most programming languages support the concept of **functions**, self-contained modules of code that perform specific tasks. Functions enable you to break a program down into small, well-defined units of code. They can be executed one or many times within a program, be executed at any time and from within many places in a program (including from other functions), and can take values for input and return a value(s) as a result of execution. Let's say, for example, that you need to perform a certain set of operations multiple times within a program. Instead of writing these instructions multiple times within the program, you write a function containing them and execute it each time the set of operations must be performed.

Swift functions are *first-class types*; what this means is that they may be assigned to variables, passed as arguments and returned as values to/from other functions, and included in other types. Every Swift function has a name, which is provided when defining a function and also used to call (i.e. execute) it. In addition, Swift functions are also *reference types*, meaning that a reference (i.e. a pointer) to a function is passed during assignment or when provided as a function argument or return value.

Definition

You describe a function with a *function definition*, a program fragment that includes all the code necessary to perform a described task. The definition specifies the function name, its input values (i.e. *parameters*), the type of each value returned as the result of function execution, and of course its executable code. The syntax for defining a function is:

Listing 7-1. Function Definition

```
func name(parameters) -> returnType {
  // Function body

}
```

A function definition is written with the `func` keyword followed by its name; zero or more function parameters enclosed in parentheses, the (optional) return type, then the code enclosed within curly braces. If a return type is provided it is separated from the parentheses enclosed parameters by the return arrow (->) symbol. The following code defines a function named `hello` with zero parameters that returns a value of type `String`:

```
func hello() -> String {
    return "Hello, world!"
}
```

You invoke a function by providing its name followed by its arguments in parentheses. The order of arguments in a function call must match the order of arguments in the function declaration. Each argument is separated by a comma, if there are no arguments then the parentheses is empty. The following example invokes the `hello()` function you defined above and assigns its returned value to the variable `greeting`:

```
var greeting = hello()
```

Let's demonstrate defining and calling a function with an example. In your playground delete any existing code and add the following:

```
func hello(name: String) -> String {
    return "Hello, \(name)!"
}

var greeting = hello("World")
```

Figure 7-1. Defining and Calling Functions

The code of Figure 7-1 demonstrates creating and using Swift functions. It defines a function named `hello` with a single parameter named `name` of type `String`. The function code uses String interpolation to insert the value of the input parameter in the returned String literal. Next the function is invoked with the input value (*World*), and the result is assigned to the variable `greeting`. You should experiment with this code (e.g. changing the input value) and observe the output in the sidebar.

Function Parameters

A function can have multiple parameters, and each parameter can have both a *local* and an *external* name.   Local parameter names are specified when defining a function, and assign the values provided when the function is invoked to the named parameters used within the body of the function implementation. External parameter names, on the other hand, are used to name arguments when a function is called. External parameter names are especially useful when a function has multiple parameters to clarify which value is applied to which parameter. The syntax for each parameter in a function definition is thus:

Listing 7-2. Function Parameters Definition

```
func functionName(extName localName: parmType, ...) {

   // Function body

}
```

As shown above, each parameter is specified with its external name (*extName*) and its local name (*localName*) followed by a colon and the parameter's corresponding type (*parmType*). The following example defines a function named sum that has two parameters of type Int and returns an Int result:

```
func sum(a1 addend1: Int, a2 addend2: Int) -> Int {

   return addend1 + addend2

}
```

Notice that the local parameter names (addend1, addend2) are used within the body of the function implementation and the external names (a1, a2) are used to name arguments when the function is invoked. You can call the function by typing in its name followed by its arguments (i.e. values) in parentheses, with each value prefaced by its external parameter name, as follows:

```
sum(a1: 5, a2: 8)
```

An explicit local parameter name must be specified for each parameter in a function definition. If you don't want to specify an external name for one or more parameters you can write an underscore (instead of an external name) for the corresponding parameter(s) in the function definition. The following example redefines the function named sum with no external parameter names:

```
func sum(_ addend1: Int, _ addend2: Int) -> Int {

   return addend1 + addend2
```

```
}
```

You can then call this version of the `sum` function (with no external parameter names) as follows:

```
sum(5, 8)
```

Function Parameter Naming Conventions

With Swift functions, by default the first parameter omits its external name, and the second and subsequent parameters use their local name as their external name. Given the above defaults the `sum(_:addend2:)` function can be defined as follows:

```
func sum(addend1: Int, addend2: Int) -> Int {
    return addend1 + addend2
}
```

You would then invoke the function as follows:

```
sum(5, addend2: 8)
```

Notice that due to the default parameter-naming conventions, when you call the function defined above its first parameter has no external name while its second parameter does.

Function Signature

A *function signature* lists a function name followed (in parentheses) by the names of each of its external parameters, each of which is delimited with a colon. If a parameter does not have an external name then an underscore (`_:`) is shown in its place. The above function named `sum` is thus described with the function signature `sum(_:addend2:)`.

Function signatures are useful for completing describing the components of a function call (its name and the names of its external parameters, in the proper order).

Default Parameter Values

You can define a default value for one or more function parameters. The value is specified in the function definition immediately after its type; the syntax for defining a default value is:

Listing 7-3. Function Default Parameter Values Definition

```
func functionName(lName: pType = defaultValue) {
    // Function body
```

```
}
```

When you supply a default value for a parameter as part of a function definition, Swift automatically provides an external name for it. To call this function you supply the parameter name with a corresponding value, or omit the parameter entirely to use the default value. As an example you can redefine the above `sum(_:addend2:)` function with a default value for the `addend2` parameter as follows:

```
func sum(addend1: Int, addend2: Int = 1) -> Int {

    return addend1 + addend2

}
```

Hence if no value is provided for the second parameter, the function returns the value of the first parameter incremented by 1. Hence with a default parameter value for the `sum(_:addend2:)` function the following statement stores a value of 8 in the variable `result`:

```
var result = sum(7)
```

Variadic Parameters

Swift functions support *variadic* parameters; in other words a function parameter that consists of zero or more values of a specific type. You write a variadic parameter in the function definition by appending three period characters (. . .) after the parameter's type name. The values for a variadic parameter are made available as an array of the specified type in the function body. Also note that a function can have at most one variadic parameter, and it must always be defined as the last parameter in the list of parameters for the function definition. The following example modifies the `sum` function to support adding zero or more values:

```
func sumAll(addends: Int...) -> Int {

    int sum = 0

    for addend in addends {

      sum += addend

    }

    return sum

}
```

You call a function with variadic parameters by providing the values as a comma-separated list, as shown here:

```
var sum = sumAll(1, 2, 3, 5, 8)
```

Function parameters are by default constants; if you want to be able to change the value of a function parameter within the body of a function you prefix the parameter name with the `var` keyword.

Function parameters by default are local and thus can only be changed within the function itself. In Chapter 5 you learned about the `inout` keyword; this is placed on a parameter within a function definition to enable its value to be changed within the function body and for those changes to persist after the function has been executed. An ampersand (`&`) is placed directly before the value when you call a function that has an in-out parameter.

Now let's demonstrate all of these concepts with an example. In your playground delete any existing code and add the following:

```
func sum(addend1: Int, addend2: Int) -> Int {
    return addend1 + addend2
}
var result = sum(5, addend2: 4)
result = sum(5)
```

Figure 7-2. Handling Function Parameters

The code shown in Figure 7-2 demonstrates use of parameters for defining and calling functions. It defines a function named `sum` with two parameters; the first has a parameter named `addend1` and the second is named `addend2`.   The first parameter has a local name, while the second has a default value. Now you call the function, the first invocation provides values for both parameters and the second only provides a value for the first parameter, thus the second parameter uses the default value.   You should experiment with this code (e.g. changing the input values) and observe the output in the sidebar.

Function Types

At the beginning of this chapter you learned that a Swift function is a first-class type. Syntactically a function type is specified as its parameter types (in parentheses), followed by the return keyword (->), and then the corresponding return type. For the sum(_:addend2:) function defined previously as:

```
func sum(addend1: Int, addend2: Int) -> Int {

   return addend1 + addend2

}
```

Its type is (Int, Int) -> Int. In other words, sum(_:addend2:) is a function type that takes two parameters of Int type and returns an Int. Because functions have all the properties of other Swift types you have learned about, they can be assigned as variables, used as a return type of another function, or used as a parameter for another function. An important benefit of using a function type as the parameter to a function is that it improves modularization of your code. It accomplishes this by enabling you to dynamically modify the behavior of a function via a function type passed as an input parameter.   The following example defines a function that uses a function type as a parameter:

```
func calculate(operation: ([Int]) -> Int, values:
Int...) -> Int {

   return operation(values)

}
```

The calculate(_:values:) function has two parameters and returns a value of type Int. The two parameters are a function type named operation that takes an array of Ints and returns an Int, and a variadic parameter named values of type Int. The body of the calculate(_:values:) function executes the function named operation (passed as an argument) and returns its result.

Thus you pass a function to calculate(_:values:), and that function is used in the body of calculate(_:values:) to perform its processing. As the function type is an input parameter, it can be chosen at run-time, thereby enabling you to dynamically change the function's overall behavior.

Now let's demonstrate the use of function types with an example. In your playground delete any existing code and add the following:

```
func calculate(operation: ([Int]) -> Int, values:
```

```
Int...) -> Int {
  return operation(values)
}
func add(addends: [Int]) -> Int {
  var sum = 0
  for addend in addends {
    sum += addend
  }
  return sum
}
func multiply(multiplicands: [Int]) -> Int {
  var product = 1
  for multiplicand in multiplicands {
    product *= multiplicand
  }
  return product
}
// Now invoke calculate function
calculate(add, values: 1, 2, 3, 5, 8)
calculate(multiply, values: 1, 2, 3, 5, 8)
```

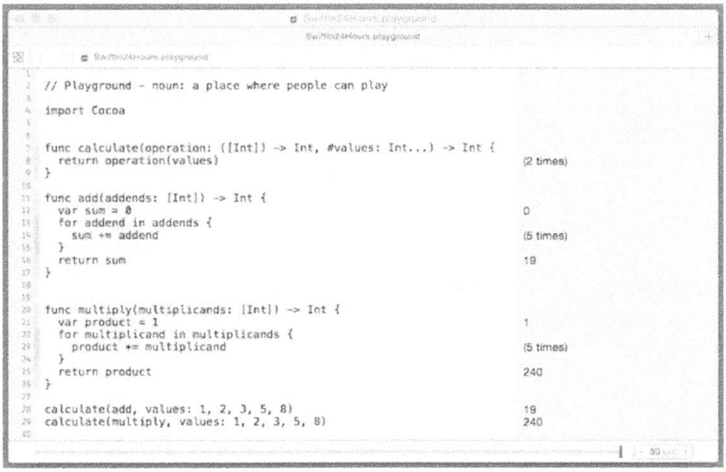

Figure 7-3. Function Types

The code shown above (displayed in Figure 7-3) demonstrates the use of function types as function parameters. The code implements three functions: a function named `calculate(_:values:)` and two additional functions named `add(_:)` and `multiply(_:)`. The `calculate(_:values:)` function will compute and return a value for zero or more input values, using the input computation function (assigned to the parameter named `operation`). The `add(_:)` function will sum the input values and return the result while the `product(_:)` function will multiply the input values and return the result. The `calculate(_:)` function is invoked using the `add(_:)` function as a parameter along with a list of input values, then the `calculate(_:values:)` function is invoked using the `multiply(_:)` function along with a list of input values. Thus you can dynamically change the behavior of the `calculate(_:values:)` function (e.g. add, multiply, etc.) based on the input function type. You should experiment with this code (e.g. changing the input values) and observe the output in the sidebar.

Nested Functions

So far, you have coded and used *global functions*, meaning functions that are defined at global scope and thus are visible throughout a program. Swift also enables you to define functions inside of other functions; these are referred to as *nested functions*. A nested function is implemented just like a standard function; however it is by default only visible within (and thus called by) its enclosing function. The following code defines a function named `greeting(_:)` that includes a nested function named `hello(_:)`:

```
func greeting(name: String) {

  func hello(user: String) -> String {

    return "Hello, \(user)"

  }

  print(hello(name))

}
```

A nested function has access to any variables defined within its enclosing function. As a result the nested function `hello(_:)` defined above can be updated as follows:

```
func greeting(name: String) {

  func hello() -> String {

    return "Hello, \(name)"

  }

  print(hello(name))

}
```

Notice how the updated version of the `hello()` function is able to use the variable `name` from its enclosing function `greeting(_:)`. An enclosing function can also return a nested function as a result, enabling them to be used in another scope.

Chapter 8

CLOSURES

In the previous chapter you learned the features and benefits of Swift functions. This chapter provides an introduction to **closures**, a powerful feature that extends the capabilities of functions by enabling you to write self-contained blocks of code that captures and stores references to variables from within the surrounding context in which it is defined. Together Swift functions and closure expressions enable you to develop code using the *functional programming* paradigm, a programming style that increases the modularity of your code.

Closure Expression Syntax

In Swift a function is in fact a special type of closure; Swift closures can come in three forms, two of which were discussed in the previous chapter:

Global functions – These are named closures that have access to values within their function body, including input parameters.

Nested functions – These are named closures that have access to values from their enclosing function.

Closure expressions – These are unnamed closures that can access variables from within their surrounding context. As closure expressions are unnamed they are written inline; the general syntax for defining a closure expression is:

Listing 8-1. Closure Expression Definition

```
{ (parameters) -> returnType in
    // Closure body

}
```

Curly braces surround the entire expression, and the closure body is provided in the statements on lines after the `in` keyword. Closure expression parameters have the same properties of function parameters except that default values cannot be provided. As with functions, closure expressions are *reference types*. Now let's demonstrate the use of closure expressions with an example. In your playground delete any existing code and add the following updated `calculate(_:_:operation:)` function:

```
func calculate(value1: Int, _ value2: Int, operation:
```

```
(Int, Int) -> Int) -> Int {

   return operation(value1, value2)

}
```

This version takes two values and a function type as arguments. Notice that the function definition does not specify an external name for the second parameter by writing an underscore next to its local parameter name (`value2`). Next let's define a closure expression to add two numbers:

```
{(a1: Int, a2: Int) -> Int in

   return a1 + a2}
```

Now you can use this closure expression as an argument to the `calculate(_:_:operation:)` function for adding two numbers:

```
var sum = calculate(25, 52, {(a1: Int, a2: Int) -> Int in

   return a1 + a2 })
```

Then use another closure expression as an argument to the `calculate(_:_:operation:)` function for multiplying two numbers:

```
var product = calculate(25, 52, {(a1: Int, a2: Int) -> Int in

   return a1 * a2})
```

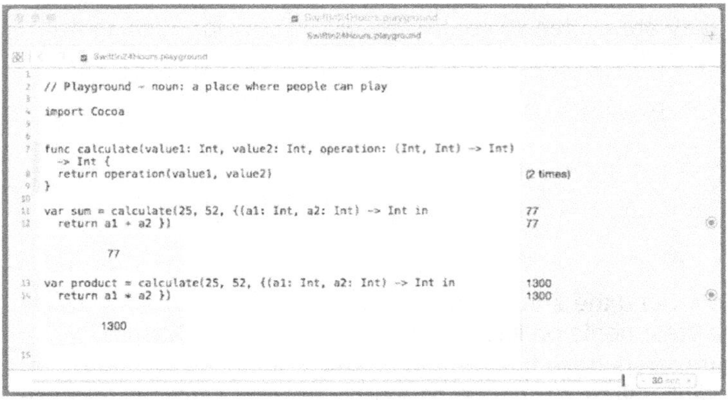

Figure 8-1. Closure Expressions

As shown in Figure 8-1, the behavior of the `calculate(_:_:operation:)` function is changed through use of an inline closure expression. You should experiment with this code (e.g.

changing the input values to the function, providing more closure expressions to subtract, divide, etc.) and observe the output in the sidebar.

Capturing Values

Earlier this chapter mentioned that closure expressions have access to, and thus *capture values* from their surrounding context. To understand what this means, let's take a moment to understand scope and visibility rules. The visibility of a variable refers to the portion(s) of a program in which it can be accessed; this is also referred to as a variable's *scope*. For example, variables declared within a Swift global function definition have *local scope,* meaning that they are visible and accessible within the function, and not accessible elsewhere. Let's illustrate this with an example; the following code will trigger a compilation error:

```
var greeting = "Hello, World!"
func hello() {
    // Illegal access of variable greeting, not within
scope
    print(greeting)

}
```

The error occurs because the variable `greeting` is not within the scope (and thus not accessible) of the function `hello()`. Nested functions have access to variables within their enclosing function. Closure expressions, on the other hand, have support for *lexical scope.* This means that closure expressions can capture variables within the surrounding scope in which they are defined. Curly braces delimit scope, and in addition scopes may be nested. Let's demonstrate how closure expressions capture values with an example. In your playground delete any existing code and add the following:

```
func hello(name: String) {
    let greeting = {() -> String in
        return "Hello, \(name)"}
    print(greeting())

}
hello("Welcome to Swift")
```

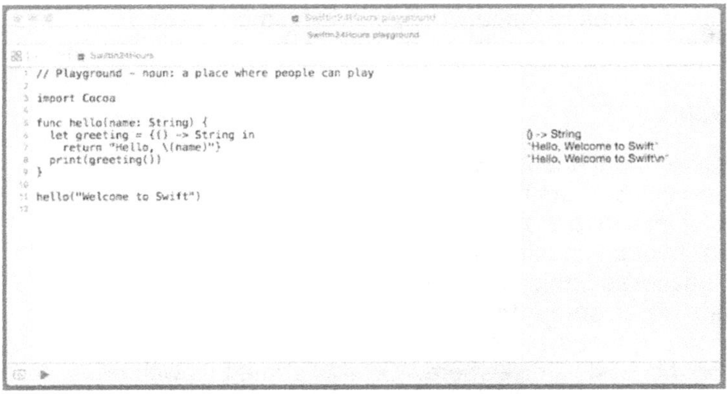

Figure 8-2. Capturing Values

The closure expression of Figure 8-2 is assigned to the variable greeting. It is defined within the scope of the enclosing function hello(_:) and thus captures its variables, in this case the parameter name. This variable is then available within the body of the closure expression and is used to create the String returned by the closure expression. Next the function hello(_:) is called with an argument which is then available to the inline closure expression. You should experiment with this code (e.g. changing the input value to the function, modifying the closure expression) and observe the output in the sidebar.

When a closure expression captures a variable, it is either captured by reference or copied by value, depending on whether or not the value of the variable is changed within the body of the expression. In the previous example from Figure 8-2, a copy of the value for name is passed to the closure expression, as its value is unchanged.

Closure Expression Optimizations

Swift provides a variety of optimizations to closure expression syntax that can make them easier to write and use. The first of these optimizations is type inference. The types of parameters and return value can be inferred from the context when passing an inline closure expression to a function as an argument. Earlier you implemented the calculate(_:_:operation:) function with a function type parameter named operation:

```
func calculate(value1: Int, _ value2: Int, operation:
(Int, Int) -> Int) -> Int {

    return operation(value1, value2)

}
```

You then invoked the function, providing an inline closure expression for the value of the parameter:

```
var sum = calculate(25, 52, {(a1: Int, a2: Int) -> Int in

    return a1 + a2 })
```

As the closure expression is a function argument, its parameter and return value types in the expression can be inferred. Thus the types do not need to be specified in the expression and the code can be rewritten as:

```
var sum = calculate(25, 52, {(a1, a2) in

    return a1 + a2 })
```

If a closure only has a single statement its result can be implicitly returned (i.e. you don't need to use the `return` keyword). The code is then further simplified to:

```
var sum = calculate(25, 52, {(a1, a2) in a1 + a2 })
```

Swift automatically provides shorthand argument names for inline closure expressions. These argument names are notated as `$0`, `$1`, `$2`, etc., and can be used to refer to the values of the closure expression's arguments, thus eliminating the need for a parameter list (and the `in` keyword) in a closure expression. Using shorthand argument names the above code becomes:

```
var sum = calculate(25, 52, { $0 + $1 })
```

Finally you can make use of *trailing closures*; a trailing closure is a closure expression that is written outside of and after the parentheses of its supporting function call. Using a trailing closure the above example becomes:

```
var sum = calculate(25, 52) { $0 + $1 }
```

Most often you would use a trailing closure when the closure is too long to fit on a single line. Let's demonstrate the above optimizations with an example; in your playground delete any existing code and use each of the closure expression optimizations presented above on the `calculate(_:_:operation:)` function.

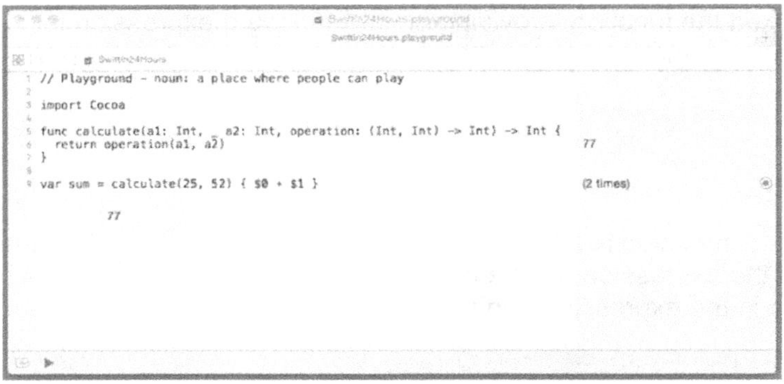

Figure 8-3. Closure Expression Optimizations

As shown in Figure 8-3, closure expression optimizations enable you to both reduce the amount of code you have to write while also clarifying your intent.

Handling Reference Cycles

As noted at the beginning of this chapter a closure is a reference type. When a closure expression captures a variable, it is either captured by reference or copied by value. Now when a closure expression captures a variable by reference and the variable itself has a reference to the expression, a *strong reference cycle* may result. A strong reference cycle occurs when two instances hold a strong reference to each other; an example of where this may occur is when a class is defined with a closure expression that accesses a property or method of the class instance itself (don't worry, you'll learn about classes in the upcoming Named Types chapter). Swift enables you to resolve strong reference cycles between a closure expression and class instance by defining a *capture list*. Such a list declares each closure expression captured reference to be a *weak* or *unowned* reference rather than a strong reference. The syntax for declaring a weak or unowned reference in a closure expression is:

Listing 8-1. Closure Expression With Weak or Unowned References

```
{ [unowned p1, weak p2, ...](parameters) -> returnType
in

    // Closure body

}
```

Notice each captured variable in the list is annotated with either the unowned or weak keyword. This represents captured reference variables (from the enclosing class instance) that are referenced in the body of the closure expression. A captured variable that will never become nil during the body of the closure expression should be annotated as an `unowned` reference, whereas a captured variable that may become `nil` should be annotated as a `weak` reference.

Chapter 9

NAMED TYPES

Just as you can define and use functions, Swift enables you to define and use custom types. A user-defined (named) type combines both data and operations that can be performed on that data. You have already become familiar with some of the Swift Standard Library named types (e.g. the numeric types, Strings, and collection classes) earlier in this book. In this chapter you'll learn how to create and use your own named types.

Modularity is a key factor in developing software efficiently and correctly. When done properly modular design can enable software independence, reuse, and efficiency through:

- **Development** of independently created components

- **Reuse** of pre-existing components

- **Efficiency** in being able to combine pre-existing components

You have already learned how Swift supports modular software design through functional programming patterns (i.e. functions and closure expressions). Swift also supports modular design via *object-oriented* programming patterns using named types.

Object-oriented programming, or OOP as it is commonly known, is a style of computer programming that emphasizes the creation and use of *software objects* to write programs. You can think of a software object as a model, in software, of a thing or concept. A software object provides a representation (in software) of the characteristics or attributes of the thing/concept being modeled along with a definition of the things it can do. The attributes (aka its *properties*) that define an object are typically things the object *has or is*; for example if you were modeling a person the set of attributes would include height and weight. The things an object can do (aka its *behaviors*), are generally the actions that it can perform (for a person object this could be things like run, jump, speak, etc.). Let's try to clarify this with an example that specifies an object-oriented model of an *atom* (e.g., hydrogen, oxygen, etc.). Now a *very* simplified model of an atom might include the following properties:

- Protons (number of protons of the atom)

- Neutrons (number of neutrons of the atom)

91

- `Electrons` (number of electrons of the atom)

You may also want to include some of the things we can do with a software model of an atom:

- `Get Element` (determine the chemical element name of the atom)

- `Get Mass` (determine the atomic mass of the atom)

- `Illustrate` (display a diagram of the atom)

- `Perform Fission` (split the atom's nucleus)

- `Create` (create an Atom object with the desired number of protons, neutrons, and electrons)

The resulting object-oriented software model for an atom is shown in Figure 9-1 below.

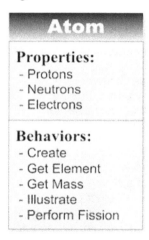

Figure 9-1. Atom Software Model

With Swift user-defined types you can create your own objects for modeling things in software, whether they are real-world entities, abstract concepts, and/or processes. This is modular design in a nutshell, and enables you to both reduce software complexity and make its structure more clear.

Elements

The Swift programming language enables you to define and use *enumeration*, *structure*, *class*, and *protocol* named types. Each type is specified by its properties and methods, and provides additional mechanisms for creating instances. The next few chapters cover these basics in more detail.

Properties

In Swift properties are used to access (i.e. get, set) the state of a named type. Swift properties can be *stored* (constant or variable values stored as part of an instance), or *computed* (calculated values). Stored properties can be defined for structures and classes, whereas computed properties can be defined for enumerations, structures, and classes. Although properties are usually associated with instances of a type, you can also define properties that are associated with a type itself. These are known as *type* properties.

You define a stored property for a user-defined type by defining a constant or variable within the body of the type definition. For a user-defined class named `Greeting` the following code defines a stored property named `salutation` of type `String`:

```
class Greeting {

  var salutation: String

  // Additional code for class definition

}
```

Note that the stored property definition is just a standard constant/variable provided within the body of a type definition. A default value for a stored property can be provided when defined or set/modified during initialization. The following code updates the `salutation` property with the default value "Hello":

```
class Greeting {

  var salutation = "Hello"

  // Additional code for class definition

}
```

Computed properties are calculated values. As such two *methods* (i.e. functions associated with a type) named `get` and `set` respectively are provided for each to retrieve and set these values.   These methods are defined by declaring the property's name and type, then defining its `get` and `set` methods within braces as follows:

```
// Definition for a computed property named
computedProp

var computedProp: propertyType {
```

```
  get {

    // Code to retrieve computedProp value

  }

  set {

    // Code to set computedProp value

  }

}
```

The following code adds a read-only computed property (i.e. it only defines a `get` method) named `description` to the `Greeting` class:

```
class Greeting {

  var salutation = "Hello"

  var description: String {

    get {

      return "Greeting with \(salutation)"

    }

  }

  // Additional code for class definition

}
```

Computed properties cannot be constants, and hence must be declared as variables. You access a property using Swift dot syntax; for instance properties you specify the name of the instance and the name of the property separated by the dot operator (`.`). For an instance of the `Greeting` class named `greeter`, the following code retrieves the value of its `salutation` stored property and assigns it to a variable named `hello`:

```
var hello = greeter.salutation
```

The next example sets the `salutation` property to the value "Greetings":

```
greeter.salutation = "Greetings"
```

The final example prints to the console the value of the instance's `description` computed property:

```
print(greeter.description)
```

A type property is also accessed using dot syntax; you specify the name of the type and the type property separated by the dot operator.

Methods

A named type can have *methods*; these are functions associated with a type. Swift provides support for both *instance methods* that belong to an instance of a named type, and *type methods* that belong to the type itself. Instance methods have implicit access to all the instance properties and methods of that type. You can define both instance and type methods for Swift enumerations, structures, and classes. For a user-defined class named `Greeting` the following code defines an instance method named `sayHello(_:)` that takes a single argument of type `String` and returns a value of type `String`:

```
class Greeting {
  var salutation = "Hello"
  func sayHello(name: String) -> String {
    return "\(salutation), \(name)!"
  }
}
```

Instance methods are called using dot syntax, as with properties. The following code calls the `sayHello(_:)` method of a `Greeting` instance named `greeter`, and assigns the result to a variable named `hello`:

```
var hello = greeter.sayHello("World")
```

Earlier in the Functions chapter you learned that function parameters could have both a local and an external name. This is also true for named type methods. As with functions, by default the first parameter omits its external name, and the second and subsequent parameters use their local name as their external name. Let's illustrate this with an example: below the `Greeting` class defined earlier has been extended with a new method whose *signature* is `sayHello(_:salute:)`:

```
class Greeting {
  var salutation = "Hello"
  // Other functionality
  func sayHello(name: String, salute: String) -> String
{
    salutation = salute
    return "\(salutation), \(name)!"
```

```
    }

}
```

Method Signatures

A method signature is analogous to a function signature, as described in the Functions chapter. It encapsulates a method name followed (within parentheses) by its external parameter names, where each name is terminated with a colon. A method signature parameter without an external name is indicated with an underscore. So taking the above example the method signature `sayHello(_:salute:)` defines a method whose name is `sayHello` and has two parameters, the first of which has no external parameter name and the second with an external parameter name of `salute`. The following code calls the `sayHello(_:salute:)` method of a `Greeting` instance named `greeter`, and assigns the result to a variable named `hello`:

```
var hello = greeter.sayHello("World", salute:
"Greetings")
```

Initializers

Swift provides initialization functionality to support the creation of instances of named types. Initialization includes memory allocation, setting of an initial value for each stored property of an instance, along with any other setup or configuration required. Each stored property of a named type must be initialized before it is used. You control this process by defining *initializers*, which are special methods defined for named types that can be called when creating instances of these types. The syntax for defining named type initializers is:

Listing 9-1. Named Type Initializer Definition

```
init(params) {

    // Initialization code

}
```

As shown above, an initializer begins with the `init` keyword, followed by zero or more method parameters within parentheses. For a user-defined class named `Greeting` the following code defines a no-argument initializer that sets an initial value for the `salutation` stored property:

```
class Greeting {

    var salutation: String

    init(){
```

```
   salutation = "Hello"

}

// Additional Greeting code

}
```

You can create an instance of a named type using *initializer syntax*, whereby you specify the name of the type followed by parentheses. If the named type has initializers with parameters, the parameter(s) for the corresponding initializer should be provided in parentheses. The following code creates an instance of the `Greeting` class using initializer syntax and assigns it to a variable named `greeter`:

```
var greeter = Greeting()
```

In summary, when the instance an instance of a named type (i.e. enumeration, structure, or class) is created, the corresponding initializer is invoked to complete initialization.

Initializer Parameter Naming Conventions

It is important to note that by default, initializers for structures and classes have an external name for every parameter that is the same as the corresponding local parameter name. This differs from the function and method parameter convention, where by default the first parameter omits its external name, and the subsequent parameters use their local name as their external name. For example, the following initializer for a class named `TestClass` has two parameters named `param1` and `param2`:

```
init(param1: String, param2: Int) {

   // Initialization code

}
```

You would create an instance of this class using initializer syntax, where each parameter is identified by its corresponding external name as follows:

```
TestClass(param1: "This is a test", param2: 1)
```

Now let's review what you've learned about properties, methods, and initializers with an example; in your playground delete any existing code and add the following:

```
class Greeting {

   var salutation = "Hello"

   var description: String {

      get {
```

```
        return "Greeting with \(salutation)"

    }

}

func sayHello(name: String) -> String {

    return "\(salutation), \(name)!"

}

func sayHello(name: String, salute: String) -> String
{

    salutation = salute

    return "\(salutation), \(name)!"

}

}

var greeter = Greeting()

greeter.sayHello("World")

greeter.description

greeter.sayHello("Pardners", salute:"Howdy")

greeter.description
```

Figure 9-2. Named Type Properties and Methods

The Greeting class shown in Figure 9-2 is defined with two properties and two methods. An initializer is not provided; however since its single stored property (salutation) has a default value, Swift automatically provides a default initializer for the class. The code creates an instance of the `Greeting` class assigned to the variable `greeter`, and then invokes its methods and accesses its properties. You should experiment with this code (e.g. changing the method parameter values) and observe the output in the sidebar.

Enumerations

The enumeration type is a collection comprised of a complete list of all possible values for variables of that type. The named values of an enumeration type are also known as enumeration members or *enumerators*. Enumerations provide an abstraction that enables you to represent in code a thing or concept that denotes a restricted set of values. For example, the seven days of the week may be modelled with an enumerator type that has members named `MONDAY`, `TUESDAY`, `WEDNESDAY`, etc.

The Swift enumeration type is a value type, meaning that it is copied on assignment and function calls. Its members can have underlying (raw) values or no values, and the raw values can be of `String`, `Character`, or one of the numeric types. Its members can also have *associated* values of any type; this enables you to store additional values with each enumerator.

Definition

You define an enumeration with the following syntax:

Listing 9-2. Enumeration Definition

```
enum EnumerationName {

    case Enumerator1Name

    case Enumerator2Name

    case Enumerator3Name

  // Additional enumerators

}
```

The `enum` keyword begins the definition of an enumeration, and the entire definition is placed within curly braces. The `case` keyword is used to indicate that a new line of enumerators is being defined. The following code defines an enumeration named `Grades` with corresponding enumerator values, each on a separate line:

```
enum Grades {

    case A
```

```
    case B

    case C

    case D

    case F

}
```

You can specify multiple enumerators on a single line, each separated by a comma. Using this approach the above enumeration is defined as:

```
enum Grades {

    case A, B, C, D, F

}
```

A new enumeration can then be created using one of its member values via dot syntax; the following code creates a `Grades` enumeration instance using the `A` member and assigns this value to the variable `grade`:

```
var grade = Grades.A
```

As you know Swift enumerations are named types, thus they can also have properties (both stored and computed), initializers, and methods. These are all specified within the body of the enumeration definition.

Raw Values

The above enumerators have no underlying *raw* values, which when provided are set to constant values for each member when an enumeration is defined. Raw values must be the same type for each member, and each value must be unique within the enumeration definition. If you use integers for raw values, they are auto-incremented if no value is specified for some of the members in the definition. The following code provides raw values for each member of the `Grades` enumeration:

```
enum Grades {

    case A = 1

    case B = 2

    case C = 3

    case D = 4

    case F = 5

}
```

The above example can also be modified to use the auto-increment feature as follows:

```
enum Grades {

    case A = 1, B, C, D, F

}
```

Associated Values

You can also provide *associated values* for one or more members of an enumeration. An associated value links a user-specified value to an enumeration instance. The enumeration definition specifies that a member has an associated value by declaring the member's type within parentheses. If there is more than one associated value for a member the corresponding types are separated by commas. The following code updates the `Grades` enumeration with an associated value of type `String` for the member named `F`:

```
enum Grades {

    case A

    case B

    case C

    case D

    case F(String)

}
```

When an instance is created for an enumeration member with an associated value it is provided within parentheses as an argument to the initializer. The following code creates a `Grades` enumeration instance with an associated value, the string `"See me after class!"`:

```
var grade = Grades.F("See me after class!")
```

The associated value is linked to the `Grades.F` enumeration member and can be retrieved via variable assignment. Associated values are commonly used to provide additional functionality to switch statements, which you'll learn next.

Enumerations with Switch Statements

Enumerations are commonly used with switch statements to control program flow. As an enumeration has a complete list of its possible values, its members can be used to provide each switch statement `case` value. For each enumeration member that has an associated value, this value can be extracted as part of the switch statement as either a constant (using the `let` prefix) or variable (using the `var` prefix). The following code demonstrates a switch statement that uses the `Grades` enumeration shown earlier with an associated value:

```
var grade = Grades.A
switch (testScore) {
  case .A:
    print("Your GPA is 4.0")
  case .B:
    print("Your GPA is 3.0")
  case .C:
    print("Your GPA is 2.0")
  case .D:
    print("Your GPA is 1.0")
  case .F(let message):
    print("Your GPA is 0.0, \(message)")
}
```

Observe the case that matches the Grades.F enumeration member assigns its associated value to a constant variable named message. This constant is then used within the corresponding case statement. OK, now let's demonstrate your use of Swift enumerations. In your playground delete any existing code and add the following:

```
enum Grades {
  case A, B, C, D, F(String)
}
func getGPA(grade: Grades) -> String {
  switch (grade) {
    case .A:
      return "Your GPA is 4.0"
    case .B:
      return "Your GPA is 3.0"
    case .C:
      return "Your GPA is 2.0"
    case .D:
      return "Your GPA is 1.0"
```

```
    case .F(let message):

        return "Your GPA is 0.0, \(message)"

    }

}

var gpa = getGPA(Grades.A)

gpa = getGPA(Grades.F("see me after class!"))
```

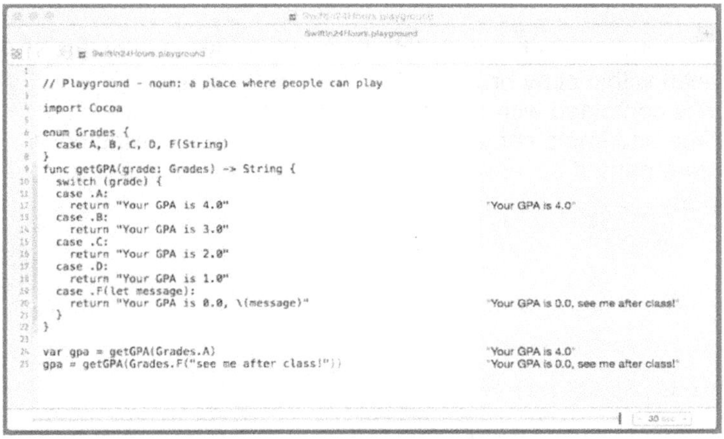

Figure 9-3. Enumerations

The getGPA(_:) function shown in Figure 9-3 uses the Grades enumeration and a switch statement (as defined earlier in this chapter) to retrieve the GPA for a corresponding grade.   It is then demonstrated for several for representative grade values. You should experiment with this code (e.g. changing the method parameter values) and observe the output in the sidebar.

Structures

A structure type is an aggregate data element that contains other values, possibly of different types, each of which is indexed by name. You have already used Swift structures in this book; for example many of the Standard Library types (such as the String and numeric types) are implemented with structures.

A Swift structure is a value type. Similar to the Swift enumeration type, you can define a structure with properties, methods, and initializers. You can define type properties and methods for a structure using the static keyword. You can also define *subscripts*; these enable you to access values using a subscript syntax, e.g. greeter[0].

Definition

You define a structure with the following syntax:

Listing 9-3. Structure Definition

```
struct StructName {
  // Structure definition
}
```

The `struct` keyword begins the definition of structure, and the entire definition is placed within curly braces. Both the interface and implementation is contained with the structure definition, i.e. there is no separate interface and implementation specification. The following code defines a structure named `Book` with three stored properties and one computed property:

```
struct Book {
  var title:String
  var author:String
  var keywords:[String] = []
  var description:String {
    get {
      return "\(title), by \(author)"
    }
  }
}
```

Structures have one or more initializers that are used to initialize the stored properties of structure instances. If a structure provides default values for all of its stored properties and does not define at least one initializer, a default initializer is automatically generated. If a structure does not provide default values for all of its stored properties and does not define at least one initializer, a *member-wise initializer* is automatically generated. This initializer takes as its parameters each of the structure's stored properties. The following code uses initializer syntax with a member-wise initializer to create a new `Book` instance assigned to a variable named `swift`:

```
var swift = Book(title: "Swift Programming Nuts and
Bolts", author: "Keith Lee")
```

You access a structure instance's properties and methods using dot syntax; the following code prints the author name for the `Book` instance named `swift` to the console:

```
print("Author \(swift.author)")
```

Mutating Methods

As you know by now, both structures and enumerations are value types. This characteristic also affects how you define methods for these types. Specifically, if a method you define for a structure or enumeration modifies one or more of its stored properties, it must be preceded with the keyword `mutating`. The following code adds a mutating method `addKeyword(_:)` to the `Book` structure; note that the method modifies the `keywords` property:

```
struct Book {

  var title:String

  var author:String

  var keywords:[String] = []

  var description:String {

    get {

      return "\(title), by \(author)"

    }

  }

  mutating func addKeyword(keyword:String) {

    keywords.append(keyword)

  }

}
```

Subscripts

Structures, enumerations, and classes can define *subscripts*; these provide a clean, concise syntax (via the subscripting operator `[]`) for accessing members of a collection or sequence in a named type. They are used to set and get values by index without having to invoke separate retrieval and update methods. For example, if the above-mentioned `Book` structure has an instance named `swift` and its `keywords` property has two entries you can access the first keyword as follows:

```
swift.keywords[0]
```

With subscripts you can define a method to access the `keywords` elements directly, e.g.:

```
swift[0]
```

or to set an element to a new value via an assignment, e.g.:

```
swift[0] = newValue
```

A subscript can take any number of input parameters, each of which can be any type. A subscript can also return any type. A type can have multiple subscript definitions, and the one used will be inferred based on the types of the value(s) within the subscript braces. You define a subscript method within a type definition using the following syntax:

Listing 9-4. Subscript Definition

```
subscript(parameters) -> returnType {
  get {
    // Code to retrieve value from collection
  }
  set(newValue) {
    // Code to set value in collection
  }
}
```

A subscript definition begins with the `subscript` keyword, followed by its parameters within parentheses, ending with its return type. A subscript can have one or more parameters, each separated by a comma. The return type is the type of the subscript value returned. The subscript method has two nested methods (named `get` and `set` respectively) to retrieve a subscript value and set a value. The code for each method is defined within curly braces, and the type of value `newValue` is the same as that of the return value (`returnType`) of the subscript. The `newValue` parameter represents the value provided for assignment when setting a value using subscripts, and is not required to be specified when defining the `set` method. The following code defines the subscript method for the `Book` structure:

```
subscript(index: Int) -> String {
  get {
    return self.keywords[index]
  }
  set(newValue) {
```

```
        self.keywords[index] = newValue
    }

}
```

In the above code the subscript parameter is of type `Int` and is used to access array elements, specifically the `keywords` property of the `Book` structure. If the keywords property were instead a dictionary with keys of `String` type, the subscript parameter would be changed accordingly. Now let's demonstrate your use of Swift structures. In your playground delete any existing code and add the following:

```
struct Book {
    var title:String
    var author:String
    var keywords:[String] = []
    var description:String {
        get {
            return "\(title), by \(author)"
        }
    }
    subscript(index: Int) -> String {
        get {
            assert((!self.keywords.isEmpty && (index >=0)),
"Index out of range")
            return self.keywords[index]
        }
        set(newValue) {
            assert((!self.keywords.isEmpty && (index >=0)),
"Index out of range")
            self.keywords[index] = newValue
        }
    }
    mutating func addKeyword(keyword:String) {
        keywords.append(keyword)
    }
```

```
}

var book = Book(title: "Swift Programming Nuts and
Bolts", author: "Keith Lee", keywords: ["Apple",
"Swift"])

book.addKeyword("Programming")

book.description

book.keywords

book[0] = "iOS"

book.keywords
```

Figure 9-4. Structures

The Book structure presented in Figure 9-4 has several properties, a subscript method, and an instance mutating method. Notice that the subscript methods uses the Standard Library assert(_:_:) function to check the value of the index before it is used to access a keywords property element. The code creates a Book instance, adds keywords via the mutating addKeyword(_:) function, and uses subscripting to get and set a keywords element. You should experiment with this code (e.g. changing the keywords parameter values and accessing different keywords elements) and observe the output in the sidebar.

Classes

The Swift class type builds on the enumeration and structure types by adding additional features to support OOP. This includes inheritance, runtime type identification, resource management, and reference counting.

Swift classes are *reference* types, meaning that a reference (i.e. a pointer) to a class instance is passed during assignment or when provided as a method argument or return value. As a result you can update the properties (i.e. state) of a reference type instance when passed into a method. This differs from value types, where a copy of a value type is passed as a parameter to a method, and hence the original instance is unchanged. You can define type properties and methods for a class using the `class` keyword.

Definition

You define a class with the following syntax:

Listing 9-5. Class Definition

```
class ClassName {
  // Class definition

}
```

The `class` keyword begins the definition of class, and the entire definition is placed within curly braces. Both the class interface and implementation is contained within this specification. The following code defines a class named `Greeting` with a computed property named `description` and a single method named `sayHello(_:)`:

```
class Greeting {
  var description: String {
    get {
      return "Greeting"
    }
  }
  func sayHello(name:String) -> String {
    return "Hello, \(name)!"
  }
}
```

Like structures, classes have one or more initializers that are used to set initial values for the stored properties of class instances. If a class does not define at least one initializer, a default initializer is automatically generated; this method takes no arguments and sets default values for all of the instance's stored properties. The following code uses initializer syntax with a default initializer to create a new `Greeting` instance assigned to a variable named `greeter`:

```
var greeter = Greeting()
```

Swift uses *Automatic Reference Counting* (ARC) for class instances, a memory management mechanism that automatically deallocates instances of Swift reference type instances when they are no longer in use, thereby freeing up resources. As a result you don't need to write code to perform manual clean up when instances are being deallocated. However, you may need to perform additional, custom cleanup when an instance is deallocated. For this purpose a class can define a *deinitializer*, a method that is called immediately before a class instance is deallocated. A class definition can have at most one deinitializer, and the syntax for defining this method is:

Listing 9-6. Class Deinitializer Definition

```
deinit {
    // Perform clean-up functions
}
```

The deinitializer begins with the `deinit` keyword, followed by the clean up code within curly braces. The following code extends the Greeting class with a simple deinitializer that just prints out a goodbye message:

```
class Greeting {
    var description: String {
        get {
            return "Greeting"
        }
    }
    deinit {
        print("Goodbye")
    }
    func sayHello(name:String) -> String {
        return "Hello, \(name)!"
    }
}
```

Inheritance

Swift classes support *inheritance*, a feature of OOP that enables you to develop a new class by extending an existing class. The new class inherits the state (properties) and behavior (methods) of the pre-existing class and can create additional properties and methods, or modify its existing specification. The new class is termed the *subclass* (or derived class) while the pre-existing class is referred to as the *superclass* (or parent class). The relationship between a superclass and a subclass is a hierarchy; as such inheritance makes it possible to create hierarchies of classes, each of which is based on a parent class. Swift supports single inheritance of both properties and methods, meaning a class can have only one parent.

You define a class based on an existing parent class with the following syntax:

Listing 9-7. Subclass Definition

```
class ClassName : SuperclassName {
  // Subclass definition
}
```

After the `class` keyword you specify the name of the new subclass, followed by a colon, the name of the existing superclass, then the definition of the subclass within curly braces. In the subclass you can modify the properties and methods of the existing superclass, and add new properties and methods as well. The following code defines a class named `Welcome` that inherits the `Greeting` class and provides an initializer for its stored property:

```
class Welcome : Greeting {
  var salutation: String
  init(greeter: String) {
    salutation = greeter
  }
}
```

A subclass can modify the instance properties, instance methods, type properties, type methods, and subscripts from the superclass it inherits. In Swift this is known as *overriding*. To override an inherited attribute in a subclass definition, you prefix the definition of the selected attribute with the `override` keyword. The following code updates the `Welcome` class by overriding the `sayHello(_:)` function defined in the superclass:

```
class Welcome : Greeting {

  var salutation: String

  init(greeter: String) {

    salutation = greeter

  }

  override func sayHello(name: String) -> String {

    return "\(salutation), \(name)!"

  }

}
```

Swift enables you to access a superclass property, method, or subscript when overriding an attribute in a subclass definition. You do this by prefixing the desired superclass attribute using the `super` prefix to specify the superclass instance, and then dot notation to specify the desired attribute. The following code overrides the description property by accessing the value of the property in the superclass to provide a custom result:

```
class Welcome : Greeting {

  var salutation: String

  init(greeter: String) {

    salutation = greeter

  }

  override var description: String {

    get {

      return super.description + " with \(salutation)"

    }

  }

  override func sayHello(name: String) -> String {

    return "\(salutation), \(name)!"

  }

}
```

Type Casting

Swift provides runtime type mechanisms that enable you to check for the type of an instance in a class hierarchy, and/or treat that instance as a different subclass or superclass within its hierarchy.

The Boolean type check operator (`is`) is used to check whether an instance is of a certain subclass type within a class hierarchy. The syntax for using the `is` operator is:

```
classInstanceName is ClassName
```

The operator returns `true` if the class instance (`InstanceName`) is an instance of the specified class (`ClassName`), or one of its subclasses. The following code creates an instance of the `Welcome` class, and then uses the type check operator to confirm it is an instance of the `Greeting` class or one of its subclasses:

```
var hi = Welcome("Hello")

var isGreeting = hi is Greeting
```

The type cast operator (`as`) is used to *downcast* an instance of a class to a subclass within the corresponding class hierarchy. The downcast can fail (for example, if you attempt to downcast an instance to a class not in its hierarchy) the operator returns an optional type. As a result, the operator comes in two forms: one of which returns an optional value (`as?`), and the other that performs the downcast and then a forced unwrapping of the value (`as!`). The forced form should only be used if you are sure the downcast will always succeed, because if it fails it throws a runtime error. The syntax for using the `as?` operator is:

```
classInstanceName as ClassName
```

The following code creates an instance of the `Greeting` class and then uses the conditional form of the type cast operator to downcast it to the `Welcome` class, and `if let` binding to retrieve the description of the new class instance:

```
var hi: Greeting = Welcome("Hello")

if let welcome = hi as Welcome {

   welcome.description

}
```

Inheritance and Initialization

Swift defines two kinds of initializers to insure proper initialization of all stored properties within a class hierarchy. *Designated initializers* fully initialize all properties defined for that class and call the appropriate superclass initializer to complete the process throughout the entire class hierarchy. Every class must have at least one designated initializer. Thus a (subclass) designated initializer must call an appropriate superclass initializer. *Convenience initializers* are secondary, supporting initializers for a class. These are optional initializers defined to simplify the creation of class instances. Convenience initializers typically set default values for some properties, and therefore reduce the number of parameters supplied when creating a new class instance. You define a convenience initializer with the following syntax:

Listing 9-8. Convenience Initializer Definition

```
convenience init(parameters) {

// Initialization code

}
```

In order to insure correct initialization when using convenience initializers, Swift has several rules, the first of which is:

1) A designated initializer must call a designated initializer from its superclass.

As noted earlier, a class with no custom initializers automatically receives a default initializer. This is always a designated initializer for a class, and thus can be used to initialize a subclass in a class hierarchy. For example, the following code adds a designated initializer to the `Welcome` class that calls the designated initializer of its superclass `Greeting`:

```
class Welcome : Greeting {

  // Other code ...

  override init() {

    super.init()

    salutation = "Hello"

  }

}
```

Notice that a designated initializer was added to the `Welcome` class and this overrides the corresponding initializer in its subclass, thus the new initializer is preceded with the **override** keyword. Also note in the `init()` method that the subclass initializer is called first, and after that the instance properties are set to their initial values. The next set of initialization rules is specific to convenience initializers:

2) A convenience initializer must call another initializer from the same class.

3) A convenience initializer must ultimately call a designated initializer.

These rules are meant to guarantee that a class instance is completely initialized for arbitrary class hierarchies when using a convenience initializer. The following code creates a convenience initializer for the `Welcome` class:

```
class Welcome : Greeting {
  // Other code ...
  convenience init(greeter: String, message: String) {
    self.init(greeter)
    print(message)
  }
}
```

Notice in the convenience initializer a designated initializer is called first, prior to other logic. Now let's demonstrate your use of Swift classes. In your playground delete any existing code and add the following:

```
class Greeting {
  var description: String {
    get {
      return "Greeting"
    }
  }
  deinit {
    print("Goodbye")
  }
  func sayHello(name: String) -> String {
    return "Hello, \(name)!"
  }
}
class Welcome : Greeting {
  var salutation: String = "Hello"
  override var description: String {
    get {
```

```
      return super.description + " with \(salutation)"
    }
  }
  init(greeting: String) {
    salutation = greeting
  }
  override init() {
    super.init()
    salutation = "Hello"
  }
  convenience init(greeting: String, message: String) {
    self.init(greeting: greeting)
    print(message)
  }
  override func sayHello(name: String) -> String {
    return "\(salutation), \(name)!"
  }
}
var greeter: Welcome = Welcome(greeting: "Greetings")
greeter.sayHello("welcome to the Swift Programming
Language")
greeter = Welcome(greeting: "Hola", message: "This is a
Test")
greeter.sayHello("World")
greeter.description
greeter = Welcome()
greeter.sayHello("Earth")
```

Figure 9-5. Classes

The `Welcome` class of Figure 9-5 is a subclass of the `Greeting` class, includes several initializers, and demonstrates overriding of properties and methods. The code creates a `Welcome` instance assigned to the variable `greeter` and invokes a method on it. Several other instances of the `Welcome` class are created using the different initializers and are each assigned to the `greeter` variable, thereby removing any reference to the previous instance and causing it to be deallocated. You should experiment with this code (e.g. changing arguments, creating more instances) and observe the output in the sidebar.

Usage Guidelines

Swift structures and classes provide very similar functionality, and thus a common question when developing Swift code is, "should I implement this code with a structure or with a class"? This paragraph provides a few guidelines that you should consider when developing named types as structures and classes.

Side Effects

As you learned earlier in this book structures are value types; as such structure instances are copied when passed as arguments to functions or methods, or when assigned to a variable. As a result, use of a structure instance in these scenarios has no *side effects* (i.e. the values of properties in the calling instance are not changed). This facilitates concurrency, because execution of the calling instance by multiple threads does not require synchronization of the structure instance. On the other hand, an entire structure instance must be copied on assignment or when passed as an argument or return value. This can impact resource utilization and performance for large structure instances.

Classes are reference types, thus the *state* (i.e. properties) of a class instance can be modified when passed as an argument to a function or method, or returned as a value. Only a reference to a class instance is passed as an argument or return value, however as a result this can cause side effects where a program's behavior may depend on its history. Reference types also enable multiple functions/methods to modify the same class instance, which must be handled properly in your code to avoid concurrency errors.

Code Reuse

Swift classes support inheritance; whereby a new class inherits the state (properties) and behavior (methods) of the pre-existing class and can create additional properties and methods, or modify its existing specification. Swift enables single class inheritance of both properties and methods, meaning a class can have only one parent.

Swift structures don't support inheritance, but provide similar code reuse via protocols and protocol extensions (you'll learn about these in the next few chapters). These language mechanisms enable you to provide a base implementation of properties and methods that can be reused by any number of structures, and are not limited to a single parent.

General Recommendations

In summary, structures should be favored when implementing flat, small to medium-sized data types where copy-by-value semantics is consistent with the problem domain. Examples of this architecture include stateless applications and applications that feature concurrent operations by multiple threads.

Classes should be favored when implementing data types with shared state where hierarchical relationships and copy-by-reference semantics are consistent with the problem domain. In addition, the Cocoa frameworks (and many 3rd party APIs) are implemented with classes, and thus you must implement subclasses to reuse and extend this functionality.

Protocols

The Swift protocol type defines a specification, in terms of declarations of properties, methods, and other requirements, that can be implemented by a named type. In this way, a protocol can be used to capture similarities among named types are not related. Any type that satisfies the requirements of a protocol (e.g., by implementing its properties, methods, etc.) *conforms* to that protocol.

Definition

You define a protocol with the following syntax:

Listing 9-9. Protocol Definition

```
protocol ProtocolName {

   // Protocol definition

}
```

The `protocol` keyword begins the definition of protocol, then its name, followed by the entire definition placed within curly braces. The following code defines a protocol named `Illustrate` that declares a property named `description` and a method named `display()`:

```
protocol Illustrate {

   var description: String { get }

   func display()

}
```

A named type indicates that it adopts a protocol in its definition by placing the protocol's name after the type's name, separated by a colon. If multiple protocols are adopted in the type definition, a comma is used to separate each. If a class adopting a protocol inherits from a superclass, the superclass name is listed before any protocols it adopts, each separated by a comma. The following code defines a class named `Welcome` whose superclass is `Greeting` and adopts the `Illustrate` protocol:

```
class Welcome: Greeting, Illustrate {

   // Class definition (including protocol)

}
```

Protocol Property Declarations

A protocol can declare both instance and type properties, each with a particular name and type. The declaration doesn't specify how a property is implemented – i.e. whether it is defined as a stored or computed property. The syntax used for declaring a protocol property is:

Listing 9-10. Protocol Property Declaration

```
protocol ProtocolName {

   var PropertyName: Type { get set }

}
```

As shown in the above property declaration, the `get` keyword indicates that the property can be read, and the `set` keyword specifies that the property is writeable. Protocol properties are always declared as variables using the `var` keyword, they cannot be declared as constants. A property must be readable, whereas write access is optional. If a property is declared as read-only, it can be implemented using a constant. If a property is writeable, it must be implemented as a variable stored property or a variable computed property. Type properties are declared in a protocol by prefixing the `var` keyword with the `static` keyword. The following code declares a read-only property named `description` of type `String` for the `Illustrate` protocol:

```
protocol Illustrate {

   var description: String { get }

   // Other declarations

}
```

Protocol Method Declarations

A protocol can declare both instance and type methods, written using the same syntax of a method definition without the method body and surrounding curly braces. Type methods are declared in a protocol by prefixing the `func` keyword with the `static` keyword. The following code declares the `display()` instance method for the `Illustrate` protocol:

```
protocol Illustrate {

   // Other declarations

   func display()

}
```

As you learned earlier in the Named Types section on Structures, enumerations and structures are value types and hence can modify their stored properties. This characteristic effects the declaration of protocol methods. If a protocol method can modify (i.e. mutate) stored properties of any named type (i.e. enumeration or structure) that can adopt the protocol, the method declaration should be preceded with the `mutating` keyword. The following code updates the `Illustrate` protocol by marking the `display()` method as mutating:

```
protocol Illustrate {

    // Other declarations

    mutating func display()

}
```

As a result, any enumeration or structure that adopts the `Illustrate` protocol can update the stored properties of the instance in the `display()` method definition.

Protocol Initializer Declarations

A protocol can declare initializers; the declaration is identical to that provided for class initializers without the initializer body and corresponding curly braces. The following code declares an initializer for the `Illustrator` protocol:

```
protocol Illustrate {

    // Other declarations

    init()

}
```

If you define a class that adopts a protocol, and one or more of the protocol's initializers can be implemented by a designated or convenience initializer, then the corresponding initializer definition(s) must be preceded with the `required` keyword. The following code defines a `Greeting` class that adopts the `Illustrate` protocol with a designated initializer:

```
class Greeting: Illustrate {

    required init() {

        // Initializer definition

    }

}
```

Protocol Types

A protocol is a first-class type; e.g. it may be assigned to variables, passed as argument and returned as a value to/from other types, or included as the type of a container such as an array, set, or dictionary.

Let's demonstrate the use of Swift protocols. In your playground delete any existing code and add the following:

```
protocol Atomic {
```

```
  var protons: UInt { get }
  var neutrons: UInt { get }
  var electrons: UInt { get }
  var atomicNumber: UInt { get }
  var atomicMass: UInt { get }
  func isNeutral() -> Bool
  init(np: UInt, nn: UInt, ne: UInt)
}
class Atom: Atomic {
  var protons: UInt = 0
  var neutrons: UInt = 0
  var electrons: UInt = 0
  var atomicNumber(): UInt {
    get {
      return protons
    }
  }
  var atomicMass(): UInt {
    get {
      return protons + neutrons
    }
  }
  func isNeutral() -> Bool {
    return protons == electrons
  }
  required init(np: UInt, nn: UInt, ne: UInt) {
    protons = np
    neutrons = nn
    electrons = ne
  }
}
```

```
var hydrogen = Atom(np:1, nn:0, ne:1)

hydrogen.atomicNumber()

var helium = Atom(np:2, nn:2, ne:2)

helium.atomicMass()

var carbonIon = Atom(np:6, nn:6, ne:7)

carbonIon.isNeutral()
```

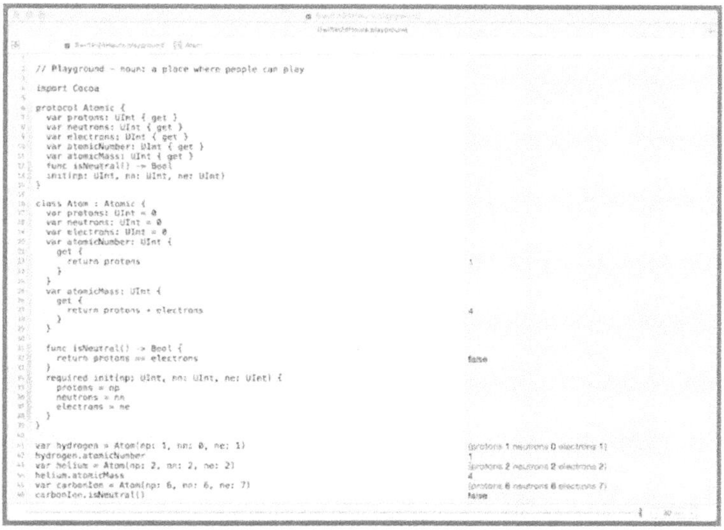

Figure 9-6. Protocols

The `Atomic` protocol of Figure 9-6 declares properties, a method, and an initializer. The `Atom` class conforms to this protocol, providing appropriate definitions for each of its requirements. The `Atom` class implements the initializer declared by the protocol as a designated initializer and thus is marked with the `required` keyword. The code creates several instances of the `Atom` class and invokes its methods accordingly. You should experiment with this code (e.g. changing arguments, creating more atom instances, etc.) and observe the output in the sidebar.

Chapter 10

EXTENSIONS

Swift extensions enable you to add new functionality to an existing enumeration, structure, class, or protocol. The new functionality becomes part of the type and, in the case of classes, is also inherited by its subclasses. Extensions can even be used on types for which you don't have the source code, such as the Swift and Cocoa APIs.

Extension Syntax

You define an extension with the following syntax:

Listing 10-1. Extension Definition

```
extension TypeName {
  // Extension functionality
}
```

An extension begins with the `extension` keyword, followed by the name of the type (e.g. enumeration, structure, class, or protocol) to which you're adding functionality. The following code begins the definition of an extension to the `Atom` class:

```
extension Atom {
  // Extension functionality
}
```

Extensions are used to add new functionality to an existing type; you cannot override existing functionality with an extension. As a result the names for extension properties, methods, etc. must be unique within the corresponding type.

Adding Functionality

Extensions can be used to add the following functionality to existing types:

- Add computed instance and type properties

- Add instance and type methods

- Add initializers

- Add subscripts

- Add and use new nested types

- Adopt and conform to a protocol

Extension Computed Properties

You can define type and instance **computed** properties in an extension –
you cannot add stored properties in an extension. In addition, if you create
a writeable computed property (via the `set` keyword), you can only store a
value via a stored property that exists in the type you are extending. The
following extension adds a computed property named
`detailedDescription` for the `Book` structure:

```
extension Book {

  var detailedDescription: String {

    get {

      return "Title: \(title), author: \(author),
description: \(description)"

    }

  }

}
```

Extension Methods

An extension can define new type and instance methods; the syntax is
identical to that used in a type definition. The following extension adds an
instance method named `addKeyword(_:)` to the `Book` structure:

```
extension Book {

  func addKeyword(keyword: String) -> String {

    keywords.append(keyword)

  }

}
```

Instance methods added with an extension can also modify the instance
itself. If an extension to a value type (i.e. a structure or enumeration)
defines a method that modifies one or more of its stored properties, it must
be preceded with the keyword `mutating`, just like mutating methods from
an original implementation. The following code modifies the previous
extension by marking the `addKeyword(_:)` method as mutating:

```
extension Book {
```

```
mutating func addKeyword(keyword: String) -> String {
    keywords.append(keyword)
  }
}
```

Extension Initializers

In an extension you can define new initializers, thereby providing additional initialization options when creating new type instances. You can define convenience initializers (prefaced with the `convenience` keyword) with a class extension; however you cannot define designated initializers or de-initializers with a class extension. The following extension for the `Book` structure defines an initializer:

```
extension Book {
    init(title: String, author: String, description:
String) {
        self.init(title: title, author: author, keywords:
[], description: description)
    }
}
```

Notice that this initializer calls the memberwise initializer of the `Book` structure. A value type (i.e. enumeration or structure) extension can only call a default or memberwise initializer if the type provides default values for all of its stored properties and doesn't define any custom initializers. A class extension initializer can call a designated or convenience initializer, in accordance with the class Inheritance and Initialization rules described earlier.

Extension Subscripts

You can define subscripts for enumerations, structures, and classes in an extension. The following extension for the `Book` structure adds a subscript for its `keywords` property:

```
subscript(index: Int) -> String {
    get {
        return self.keywords[index]
    }
    set(newValue) {
        self.keywords[index] = newValue
```

```
    }

}
```

Extension Nested Types

Extensions can add new, nested types to existing enumerations, structures, and classes. The following extension for the `Book` structure defines a nested type enumeration named `Category` that lists possible book categories:

```
extension Book {

  enum Category {

    case Fiction, Non-Fiction, Art, Philosophy, Travel

  }

}
```

Adopting a Protocol in an Extension

An extension can be used to adopt and conform to a protocol. When used in this manner all the properties, methods, etc. of the protocol are implemented in the extension. The syntax for extending a type to adopt a protocol is:

Listing 10-2. Extension Adopting a Protocol Definition

```
extension TypeName: ProtocolName {

  // Protocol implementation

}
```

The following code defines a protocol named `ISBNType` with a single read-only property named `createISBN`, and a corresponding extension to the `Book` structure that adopts the `ISBNType` protocol:

```
protocol ISBNType {

  func createISBN() -> String

}

extension Book: ISBNType {

  func createISBN() -> String {

    return "a-bcd-efgh-ijkl-m"

  }

}
```

Now let's demonstrate the use of Swift extensions for adding the above functionality. In your playground delete any existing code and add the following:

```swift
struct Book {

  var title: String

  var author: String

  var keywords: [String] = []

  var description: String

}
protocol ISBNType {

  func createISBN() - > String

}
extension Book {

  var detailedDescription: String {

    get {

      return "Title: \(title), Author: \(author),
Description: \(description)"

  }

  mutating func addKeyword(keyword: String) -> String {

    keywords.append(keyword)

  }

  init(title: String, author: String, description:
String) {

    self.init(title: title, author: author, keywords:
[], description: description)

  }

  subscript(index: Int) -> String {

    get {

      assert((!self.keywords.isEmpty && (index>=0),
"Index out of range")

      return self.keywords[index]

    }

    set(newValue) {
```

```
        assert((!self.keywords.isEmpty && (index>=0),
"Index out of range")

        self.keywords[index] = newValue

    }

  }

}

extension Book: ISBNType {

  func createISBN() -> String {

    return "a-bcd-efgh-ijkl-m"

  }

}
```

```
var book = Book(title: "Swift Programming Nuts and
Bolts", author: "Keith Lee", description: "This book
provides a comprehensive overview of the Swift
programming language")

book.detailedDescription

book.addKeyword["Swift"]

book[0]

book.createISBN()
```

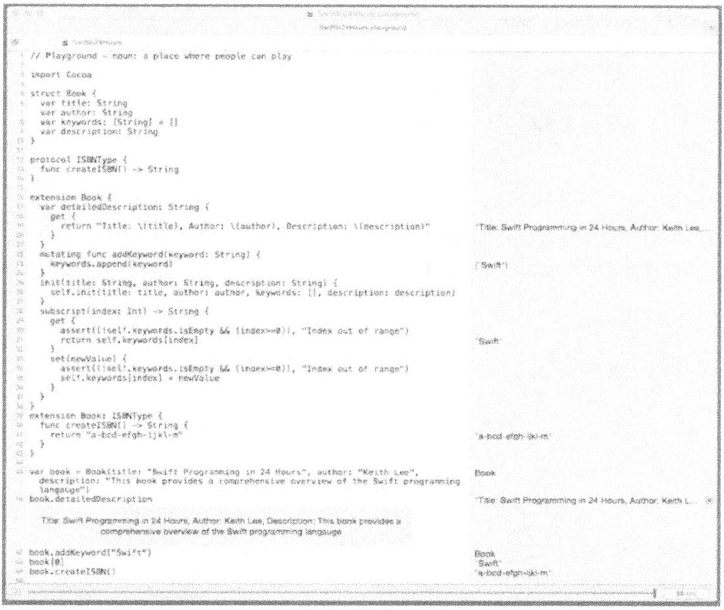

Figure 10-1. Extensions

The code of Figure 10-1 begins by defining a `Book` structure that declares several properties. Next it defines an `ISBNType` protocol that declares a single method named `createISBN()`. The first `Book` extension implements an additional property, method, initializer, and subscript for the structure. The second `Book` extension conforms to the `ISBNType` protocol, providing an appropriate definition for the `createISBN()` method. The code then creates an instance of the `Book` structure and invokes its methods accordingly. You should experiment with this code (e.g. changing arguments, creating more `Book` instances, etc.) and observe the output in the sidebar.

Protocol Extensions

In the previous section you learned how to add new functionality to a named type by implementing extensions. Swift even enables you to add new functionality to *protocols* using extensions. Using a protocol extension you can add new functionality to a protocol, and provide default implementations for a protocol's existing properties and methods. As a result, types that conform to these protocols automatically receive this custom functionality, thus extending their use and applicability. The syntax for writing a protocol extension is:

Listing 10-3. Protocol Extension Definition

```
extension ProtocolName {

    // New functionality or default implementations for
    properties and methods

}
```

The following code defines a protocol extension for the ISBNType protocol that adds a new instance method called getBarcodeImage():

```
extension ISBNType {

    func getBarcodeImage() -> [UInt8] {

        // Functionality to return barcode image file

    }

}
```

Thus any type that adopts the ISBNType protocol receives the new getBarcodeImage() method. A protocol extension can also provide default implementations of an existing protocol's properties and methods. The following code defines a default implementation of the createISBN() method for the ISBNType protocol.

```
extension ISBNType {

    func createISBN() -> String {

        return "a-bcd-efgh-ijkl-m"

    }

}
```

Types that conform to the ISBNType protocol receive the default implementation provided in the extension, therefore removing the need to define one. Note that if a conforming type provides its own implementation of a required method or property, that implementation will be used instead of the one provided by the extension.

Adding Constraints

Normally the functionality of a protocol extension is available to all types that conform to the protocol. However Swift enables you to set constraints on a protocol extension, thereby controlling which (protocol conforming) types have the functionality. A constraint is set on a protocol extension using a where clause written after the name of the protocol being extended; the syntax is:

Listing 10-5. Protocol Extension With Constraints Definition

```
extension ProtocolName where TypeName :
ConstraintProtocols {

   // Extension definition

}
```

As shown above, the `where` clause is written as a type, followed by a colon, then one or more protocols (each separated by a comma) that define the constraints. The type in a `where` clause is often specified using the `Self` type, which represents a placeholder for the type that's going to conform to that protocol. In other words, if the type conforming to the protocol extension also conforms to the protocol(s) specified in the `where` clause, it has access to the extension's default implementations. This enables you to easily extend the functionality of types through protocol conformance. As an example, the following code defines two protocols named `BookType` and `CoverType`:

```
protocol BookType {

   var title: String { get }

   var author: String { get }

   var description: String { get }

}

protocol CoverType {

   var coverImage: String { get }

}
```

Now we can define an extension for the `CoverType` that uses a constraint to control which types have access to the functionality implemented in the extension:

```
extension CoverType where Self : BookType {

   var coverImage: String {

     get {

       return "\(self.title).png"

     }

   }

}
```

The `CoverType` extension uses a `where` clause with a constraint on the

Self type to control which type instances conforming to the CoverType have access to the default implementations provided by the extension. The following where clause limits the types to those that implement the BookType protocol:

```
where Self : BookType
```

This means that the CoverType extension has access to the properties and methods specified for BookType implementations. Now let's illustrate the use of protocol extensions with an example; in your playground modify your existing code as shown in Figure 10-1 with the following:

```
protocol BookType {
    var title: String { get }
    var author: String { get }
    var description: String { get }
}
protocol CoverType {
    var coverImage: String { get }
}
extension CoverType where Self : BookType {
    var coverImage: String {
      get {
        return "\(self.title).png"
      }
    }
}
struct Book: BookType, CoverType {
    var title: String
    var author: String
    var keywords: [String] = []
    var description: String
}
extension Book {
    init(title: String, author: String, description:
String) {
```

```
    self.init(title: title, author: author,
description: description, keywords: [])

  }

}
```

```
var book = Book(title: "Swift Programming Nuts and
Bolts", author: "Keith Lee", description: "This book
provides a comprehensive overview of the Swift
programming language")
```

```
book.coverImage
```

Figure 10-2. Protocol Extensions

First the code displayed in Figure 10-2 defines two protocols, `BookType` and `CoverType`. Next the code defines a `CoverType` extension that includes a default implementation for the `coverImage` property. As this extension contains a `where` clause for types that conform to the `BookType` protocol, it has access to its `title` property. The `CoverType` extension implementation uses this to return an appropriate value for the `coverImage` property. Next the `Book` structure conforms to these protocols by defining the properties specified in the `BookType` protocol; it obtains the `coverImage` property (and its default implementation) via the `CoverType` extension. The code then demonstrates creation of a `Book` instance and accessing its `coverImage` property, provided via the protocol extension. As demonstrated in this example, the functionality implemented by a protocol extension is immediately available to any type that conforms to the protocol. Therefore multiple types (e.g. enumerations, structures, and classes) can be "decorated" with the new functionality in this way. In addition, because named types can conform to multiple protocols, protocol extensions enable you to add behaviors for multiple protocols. Together, protocols and protocol extensions are the basis for *Protocol-Oriented Programming*, a powerful new programming style that can significantly impact how you design and implement software.

Chapter 11

GENERICS

Generic programming is a style of computer programming that enables you to create software that is *parameterized with respect to types*. This abstraction can make you a more efficient and productive programmer by both reducing code duplication and also decreasing programming errors. For example, consider the following function named `swapInts(_:_:)` that exchanges the values of two variables of integer type:

```
func swapInts(inout item1: Int, inout item2: Int) {

    let temp = item1

    item1 = item2

    item2 = temp

}
```

Now if you want to exchange two variables of a different type, for example the `String` type, you have to write a new function:

```
func swapStrings(inout item1: String, inout item2:
String) {

    let temp = item1

    item1 = item2

    item2 = temp

}
```

If you want to exchange two variables of yet another type, again you have to write a new function. In effect, even though the functionality is identical in each case, you have to duplicate it for each type supported. Generics solve this problem so that you can parameterize code with respect to the type(s) specified when the functionality is utilized, thereby eliminating code duplication. With Swift support for generics the above function can be written as follows:

```
func swap<T>(inout item1: T, inout item2: T) {

    let temp = item1

    item1 = item2

    item2 = temp
```

}

Swift provides support for the creation of both generic functions and generic types, thereby reducing the number of functions and types you have to create and maintain. In addition to the elimination of code duplication, generics also preserve type safety, thereby avoiding runtime type checks and type casting. Generics are one of the language's most powerful features, and much of the Swift Standard Library uses generics. In this chapter you'll learn how to develop generic functions and types in Swift.

Generic Functions

Swift's support for the creation of generic functions enables you to define functions and closure expressions that work with any type. The syntax for defining a generic function differs from the standard function definition as follows:

Listing 11-1. Generic Function Definition

```
func name<Type Parameters>(parameters) -> returnType {
    // Function body
}
```

The type parameters, declared within angle brackets immediately after the function name, are used to specify and name placeholder types that are substituted for later when you invoke the function with the actual type. The swap(_:_:) function introduced one parameterized type within angle brackets named T:

```
func swap<T>(inout item1: T, inout item2: T) {
    let temp = item1
    item1 = item2
    item2 = temp
}
```

Type parameters are used to define a function's parameter type(s), return type, or as a type annotation within the body of the function. The type parameter(s) is replaced with the actual type when the function is called. The following code invokes the generic swap(_:_:) function on two integer values:

```
var value1 = 5
var value2 = 10
```

```
swap<Int>(&value1, &value2)   // Now value1 = 10, value2
= 5
```

Notice in the above function call the type parameter `Int` is specified in angle brackets after the function name. When you define a generic function, the name you provide for a placeholder type can be simple (i.e. a single uppercase character `T` as in the example above) or more descriptive. In either case it is recommended that the name be written with upper camel case notation, to clarify in the code that it is a placeholder for a type, not a type instance.

Let's demonstrate the use of generic functions. In your playground delete any existing code and add the following:

```
func swap<T>(inout item1: T, inout item2: T) {
    let temp = item1
    item1 = item2
    item2 = temp
}
var value1 = "Hello"
var value2 = "Goodbye"
swap(&value1, &value2)
value1
value2
```

Figure 11-1. Generic Functions

The `swap(_:_:)` function shown in Figure 11-1 interchanges two values, using generics to enable declaration of the type of the values at function invocation. The code creates the values and invokes the function, then displays the new values. You should experiment with this code (e.g. changing both the type parameter and the supplied values) and observe the output in the sidebar.

Generic Types

Swift enables you to create generic types for enumerations, structures, and classes. The syntax for defining a generic type is identical to the standard type definition, with the addition of the type parameter(s) (declared within angle brackets) placed immediately after the type name. The following provides a pseudo-code definition for a generic class called `Bag`:

```
class Bag<T> {
    init() { … }
    init(elements: Bag<T>) {…}
    func contains(item: T) -> Bool {…}
    func get(item: T) -> T? {…}
    func add(item: T) {…}
    func remove(item: T) {…}
}
```

Each type parameter is used to define a parameterized type for a custom type anywhere within its definition, e.g. for the custom type's properties, methods, initializers, etc. The type parameter(s) is replaced with the actual type(s) when an instance of the type is created. The following code creates a `Bag` instance that holds integer values:

```
var bag = Bag<Int>()
```

Associated Types

Associated types are used to parameterize types within a protocol definition. They work by giving a placeholder name (i.e. alias) to a type that is used as part of a protocol. Multiple aliases can be specified, each with its own name. The actual type(s) is not specified until the protocol is adopted. A placeholder name is specified using the `typealias` keyword. The following code modifies the `BookType` protocol from the previous chapter by adding an associated type for the `keywords` property:

```
protocol BookType {
    typealias ItemType
    var title: String { get }
    var author: String { get }
```

```
    var description: String { get }

    var keywords: [ItemType]

}
```

Next the `Book` structure conforms to the protocol, specifying the associated type `ItemType` to be of type `String`, which is inferred when the type parameter of the keywords property is specified:

```
struct Book: BookType, CoverType {

    typealias ItemType = String

    var title: String

    var author: String

    var keywords: [ItemType] = []

    var description: String

}
```

Generic Type Constraints

Swift enables you to define *type constraints* on generic functions and types, thus controlling which type parameters can be used when invoking generic functions or creating generic type instances. Specifically the constraint controls whether a generic type parameter inherits from a specific class, or conforms to a specific protocol(s). The syntax for applying a type constraint on a generic function where the type inherits from a class is:

Listing 11-2. Generic Function With Class Type Constraints Definition

```
func name<T: ParentClass>(parameters) -> returnType {

    // Function body

}
```

and the syntax if the type conforms to a specific protocol(s) is:

Listing 11-3. Generic Function With Protocol Type Constraints Definition

```
func name<T: Protocol(s)>(parameters) -> returnType {

    // Function body

}
```

You apply a type constraint on a generic type in a similar manner, with the constraint placed within angle brackets after the type name. Now let's demonstrate the use of generic type constraints with an example; in your playground delete an existing code and add the following:

```
protocol BagType {
  typealias ElementType
  func contains(item: ElementType) -> Bool
  func isEmpty() -> Bool
  func size() -> Int
  func get(item: ElementType) -> ElementType?
  mutating func add(item: ElementType)
  mutating func remove(item: ElementType)
}


struct Bag<T: Hashable>: BagType {
  var elements: Dictionary<T, T>
  init() {
    self.elements = [:]
  }
  init(items: Bag<T>) {
    self.elements = items.elements
  }
  func contains(item: T) -> Bool {
    return elements[item] != nil
  }
  func isEmpty() -> Bool {
    return elements.isEmpty
  }
  func size() -> Int {
    return elements.count
  }
  func get(item: T) -> T? {
    return elements[item]
  }
```

```
  mutating func add(item: T) {
    elements[item] = item
  }
  mutating func remove(item: T) {
    elements.removeValueForKey(item)
  }
}


var bagONames = Bag<String>()
bagONames.add("Curly")
bagONames.add("Larry")
bagONames.size()
bagONames.contains("Curly")
var bagONumbers = Bag<Int>()
bagONumbers.add(123)
bagONumbers.isEmpty()
```

Figure 11-2. Generic Type Constraints

The code of Figure 11-2 begins by defining a `BagType` protocol that
specifies requirements for several methods, along with a type alias. Next
the generic `Bag` structure conforms to the `BagType` protocol, specifying a
type constraint that mandates instances of the `Bag` type can only be
created using a type parameter that conforms to the `Hashable` protocol.
This means that items in a `Bag` instance can be stored as the keys of a
Swift `Dictionary`. Some types that conform to the `Hashable` protocol
include the Swift `String` and numeric types. Next the code creates
several instances of the `Bag` structure with different type parameters and
invokes its methods accordingly. You should experiment with this code
(e.g. changing arguments, creating more atom instances, etc.) and
observe the output in the sidebar.

ERROR HANDLING

Let's face it; errors are a significant part of the software development life cycle. In fact, how your code deals with errors is critical to implementing quality software. Runtime errors that impact the operation or performance of a program can be due to a variety of causes, such as incorrect user input, system issues, or programming errors. In this chapter you'll learn how to use Swift's mechanisms and APIs for detecting and handling recoverable errors at runtime.

Representing Errors

The `ErrorType` protocol is used to create error instances that encapsulate detected runtime error conditions. Enumerations are typically used to implement the protocol, with associated values to provide detailed information on the error condition. The following code defines an enumeration named `AccountError` that conforms to the `ErrorType` protocol:

```
enum AccountError: ErrorType {

    case InvalidAccount

    case UnknownAccount

    case TransferFundsError(message: String)

    case WithdrawFundsError(message: String)

    case DepositFundsError(message: String)

}
```

When your code detects a recoverable runtime error condition, it creates an `ErrorType` instance that represents the specifics of the condition. The Foundation Framework `NSError` class conforms to the `ErrorType` protocol, thereby enabling existing functionality (such as the Cocoa frameworks) that uses `NSError` instances to work within the Swift error handling framework.

Throwing Errors

Each function, closure, or method that can throw an error must be marked accordingly in its definition. This is specified with the `throws` keyword, which is placed in the corresponding declaration between its parameters and return type (immediately prior to the curly brace signifying the beginning of its statement body). The following code defines a protocol named `BankAccountType` with methods that can throw errors:

```
protocol BankAccountType {

    func getBalance(account: UInt) throws -> Double

    func deposit(account: UInt, amount: Double) throws ->
Double

    func withdraw(account: UInt, amount: Double) throws -
> Double

    func transfer(fromAccount: UInt, fromAmount: Double,
toAccount: UInt, toAmount: Double) throws -> Double

}
```

If your code detects a runtime error condition you signal it by throwing an error using the `throw` keyword, followed by the name of the error instance that encapsulates information about the error. Note that you can only throw an error within the body of a method, function, or closure that has been defined to support throwing errors (per its `throws` keyword explained above). The following code throws an error in the `getBalance(_:)` method of the `BankAccount` structure if its `account` input argument has a value of zero:

```
struct BankAccount: BankAccountType {

    func getBalance(account: UInt) throws -> Double {

        guard account != 0 else {

            throw AccountError.InvalidAccount

        }

        // logic to retrieve account balance

    }

}
```

Conversely, when your code invokes a function, closure, or method that can throw an error, you must preface the call with the `try` keyword. This makes it explicit that the function can throw an error and that, if thrown, a transfer of control occurs; as such the code immediately following the function may not be run. The following code invokes the `getBalance(_:)` method on an `BankAccount` instance, prefacing the call with the `try` keyword accordingly:

```
var bankAccount = BankAccount()
```

```
var currentBalance = try
bankAccount.getBalance(1234321)
```

Handling Errors

You've learned how to represent, create, and throw errors when your code detects runtime error conditions. Next you'll learn how to catch and handle errors in your code. When your code throws an error it causes a transfer of control from the current scope to the first outer scope capable of handling the error. This is accomplished by wrapping the call to a function that throws an error using a `do-catch` statement whose syntax is:

Listing 12-1. Do-Catch Statement Definition

```
do {

  // Code which calls a function that can throw error

  // Additional code executed if no error thrown

}

catch ErrorType instances {

  // Error handling code

}
```

As shown above each function, closure, or method that can throw an error is wrapped in a `do-catch` statement. A `do` statement is used to create a containing scope that can be used to transfer control to `catch` clauses for one or more error conditions. The syntax for a `do` statement is:

```
do {

  // Statements

}
```

A `catch` clause is specified after a `do` statement for each possible `ErrorType` instance, hence the number of `catch` clauses is a function of the number of different `ErrorTypes` that can be thrown by a function. The list of caught errors must be exhaustive and, as with the `switch` statement, pattern matching support is provided. The following code invokes the `getBalance(_:)` method on a `BankAccount` instance, and wraps the call in an appropriate `do-catch` block:

```
var bankAccount = BankAccount()

let account = 0

do {
```

```
    var currentBalance = try
bankAccount.getBalance(account)

}

catch AccountError.InvalidAccount {

    print("Account number invalid, please try again")

}
```

As mentioned earlier, when an error is thrown, program execution transfers from the current scope to the first outer scope capable of handling the error. In scenarios where errors can be thrown, the error handling framework also includes support for executing cleanup code via a `defer` statement. This statement can be used to perform any cleanup actions (e.g. closing files, network connections, etc.) that should be done whether or not an error has occurred. The syntax for using the `defer` statement is:

Listing 12-2. Defer Statement Definition

```
defer {

    // Code that performs cleanup actions

}
```

Code placed within the body of the defer statement is run when the current scope is exited – for example immediately prior to returning from a function call. The body of the `defer` statement cannot contain transfer-of-control statements (e.g. `continue` or `return`) nor can it contain code that throws errors.

Now let's demonstrate the use of Swift error handling functionality with an example; in your playground delete an existing code and add the following:

```
enum AccountError: ErrorType {

    case InvalidAccount

    case UnknownAccount

    case InvalidDeposit(message: String)

}

class BankAccount {

    var currentBalance = 0.0

    var accountNumber: UInt

    init(account: UInt) {
```

```
      accountNumber = account
   }
   func getBalance(account: UInt) throws -> Double {
      guard account != 0 else {
         throw AccountError.InvalidAccount
      }
      guard accountNumber == account else {
         throw AccountError.UnknownAccount
      }
      return currentBalance
   }
   func deposit(account: UInt, amount: Double) throws ->
Double {
      guard account != 0 else {
         throw AccountError.InvalidAccount
      }
      guard accountNumber == account else {
         throw AccountError.UnknownAccount
      }
      guard amount > 0 else {
         throw AccountError.InvalidDeposit("Deposit amount
must be greater than $0.00")
      }
      currentBalance += amount
      return currentBalance
   }
}


var bankAccount = BankAccount(account: 1234321)
do {
   var balance = try bankAccount.getBalance(1234321)
   balance = try bankAccount.deposit(1234321, amount:
```

```
25.75)

   try bankAccount.deposit(0, amount: 50.00)

}

catch AccountError.InvalidAccount {

   "Invalid account number, please try again"

}

catch AccountError.UnknownAccount {

   "Unknown account number, please try again"

}

catch AccountError.InvalidDeposit(let message) {

   message

}
```

Figure 12-1. Error Handling

The code shown in Figure 12-1 begins by defining an `AccountError` enumeration that conforms to the `ErrorType` protocol. This enumeration encapsulates all the error conditions that can be detected. Next the code defines a `BankAccount` class that includes several methods that can throw `AccountError` instances if runtime errors are detected. The code then creates a `BankAccount` instance and invokes its methods wrapped in a `do-catch` statement. You should experiment with this code (e.g. changing arguments to cause the different runtime errors, etc.) and observe the output in the sidebar.

Chapter **13**

RESOURCES

There are a variety of resources available to help you while you learn to program using Swift. Here you will learn about tools that you can access directly from Xcode, along with reference sources that will be of benefit along the way.

Documentation Viewer

The Xcode Documentation Viewer provides comprehensive information for developing iOS, watchOS, and OS X apps using Xcode. It includes programming guides, tutorials, sample code, detailed framework API references (including the Swift APIs), and video presentations. The information displayed by the viewer is dynamically updated when new/updated information becomes available; as such you always have access to the most recent documentation. You use the Xcode Documentation Viewer from the Xcode main menu by selecting **Window > Documentation and API Reference**. This displays the Documentation Viewer shown below in Figure 13-1.

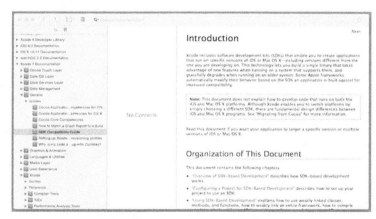

Figure 13-1. Xcode Documentation Viewer

You can use the *Search documentation* field to find the document of interest (e.g. **The Swift Programming Language** guide, etc.). The document is opened in the view in HTML format, and the left sidebar contains the Table of Contents for the opened document to ease navigation. You can browse the list of Apple developer documentation by clicking on the document library button at the top of the left sidebar, and display your bookmarks by clicking the bookmark button. You can also find information about an API by typing its name in the search field. The API reference for the API is displayed in the viewer.

Quick Help

Xcode **Quick Help** offers concise reference documentation for your code's symbols (i.e. types), build settings, and interface objects. You can display Quick Help information using the Quick Help inspector, or inline using a Quick Help window. You display the Quick Help inspector (shown in Figure 13-2) in the Quick Help pane (located in the Utility area on the right side of an Xcode workspace/playground window) by selecting **View > Utilities > Show Quick Help Inspector** from the Xcode main menu.

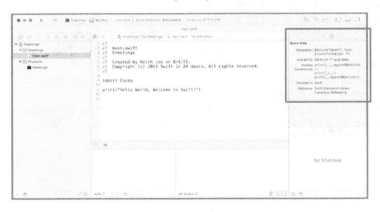

Figure 13-2. Displaying the Quick Help Inspector

Once you have opened the inspector, the Quick Help pane displays summary information and links to related resources (including sample code) on the symbol you are typing. The Quick Help pane also displays this info if you click on a symbol, build setting, or interface object.

Alternatively, you can display Quick Help info inline using a Quick Help popup window. This can be done from a playground or within the editor area of a project. When you see the desired symbol in your code, hold down the option key while hovering over the API. You should see a question mark cursor under the symbol as displayed in Figure 13-3.

Figure 13-3. Selecting a Symbol Using Quick Help Windows

Clicking on this hyperlink brings up a small popover window with Quick Help info on the symbol (shown in Figure 13-4).

Figure 13-4. Displaying a Quick Help Window

You can also use Quick Help to annotate your code and create reference documentation for your custom APIs. More information on this is provided in the Xcode **HeaderDoc User Guide**.

References

Below are references to some valuable resources for Swift application development. Keep in mind that there are plenty of other resources available to assist you, along with numerous users groups and Swift developer communities. More are coming on line all the time, so use your favorite search engines to find additional items of interest.

Documents

The Swift Programming Language (www.developer.apple.com)

Swift Standard Library Reference (www.developer.apple.com)

Swift Standard Library Functions Reference (www.developer.apple.com)

Swift Standard Library Operators Reference (www.developer.apple.com)

Swift Standard Library Type Aliases Reference
(www.developer.apple.com)

Start Developing iOS Apps (Swift) (www.developer.apple.com)

Using Swift with Cocoa and Objective-C (www.developer.apple.com)

Tutorials

Stanford University: Developing iOS 9 Apps with Swift

Plymouth University: iOS Development in Swift

Udemy: Swift: Learn Apple's New Programming Language by Examples

Treehouse: Learn Swift

Bloc: Learn Swift

Websites

Apple Developer Forums (http://devforums.apple.com)

Documentation for Swift (http://swiftdoc.org)

Helpful Resources to Learn Swift (http://learnswift.tips)

Official Swift Blog (www.developer.apple.com/swift/blog)

Chapter 14

NeXT STEPS

Whew, done with a few minutes to spare! I know that this was a lot to cover in a short amount of time, so thanks for hanging in there. Some additional topics you'll want to explore as you gain more experience with Swift include:

Advanced operators – In addition to the operators you learned about earlier in this book, Swift also defines several advanced operators that can be used to perform more complex data manipulation.

Operator overloading – Swift provides language mechanisms that enable you to define custom implementations of existing operators for selected classes and structures.

Access control – Swift provides access control mechanisms that can be used to restrict access to parts of your code from code in other source files and modules.

Dynamic types – Swift provides the `Any` and `AnyObject` types for working with *dynamic types*, that is, type instances whose actual underlying type is determined at runtime. Dynamic types are most commonly employed when using C and Objective-C code in Swift programs.

Availability checking – Swift has built-in availability checking mechanisms that make it easier to build the best possible app for each target operating system (OS) version. The compiler will give you an error when using an API too new for your minimum target OS. The `#available` keyword lets you wrap blocks of code in a conditional version check to run only on specific OS releases. The `@available` attribute can be used to add availability information to functions, methods, and named types.

You can learn more about these and other topics related to Swift programming by visiting the references listed in the above Resources chapter. Please feel free contact me on the web at http://www.motupresse.com or via email at SwiftNutsAndBolts@motupresse.com with comments on the book, for access to the example code, or to obtain book updates and corrections as they become available.

You now have a solid foundation with the Swift programming language and understand its key features and benefits. Congratulations, you are ready to begin developing iOS, watchOS, and OS X apps using Swift, enjoy the experience!

Index

About the Author

Keith Lee is a Technologist who has been implementing IT solutions and systems for over 20 years. He has a wide range of experience developing mobile, desktop, and web applications, and implementing distributed software systems.

Other titles by Keith Lee:

iOS Programming Nuts and Bolts

Objective-C Programming Nuts and Bolts

Pro Objective-C

Programming for Everyone

Connect with the Author online at:

Motu Presse: http://www.motupresse.com

Email: SwiftNutsAndBolts@motupresse.com

www.ingramcontent.com/pod-product-compliance
Lightning Source LLC
Chambersburg PA
CBHW070949050326
40689CB00014B/3401